THE
ICE CREAM
SANDWICHES
BOOK

THE
ICE CREAM
SANDWICHES
BOOK

50 recipes
for incredibly cool treats

DONNA EGAN
of
buttercup
cake shop

EBURY
PRESS

For my daughters, Audrey and Amelia:
often patient, usually encouraging, always inspiring.

10 9 8 7 6 5 4 3 2 1

Published in 2012 by Ebury Press, an imprint of Ebury Publishing

A Random House Group Company

The Random House Group Limited Reg. No. 954009

Addresses for companies within the Random House Group can be found
at www.randomhouse.co.uk

A CIP catalogue record for this book is available from the British Library

The Random House Group Limited supports The Forest Stewardship Council® (FSC®),
the leading international forest certification organisation. Our books carrying the FSC
label are printed on FSC® certified paper. FSC is the only forest certification scheme
endorsed by the leading environmental organisations, including Greenpeace. Our paper
procurement policy can be found at www.randomhouse.co.uk/environment

To buy books by your favourite authors and register for offers visit www.randomhouse.co.uk

Project editor: Ione Walder
Design: Friederike Huber
Photography: William Reavell
Food stylist: Denise Smart
Prop stylist: Jessica Georgiades
This book is based on an original idea by Haldane Mason Lt

Printed and bound by C & C Offset Printing Co., Ltd

ISBN 9780091948641

CONTENTS

Introduction   7

Decadent   10

Fresh 'n' Fruity   30

Kidelicious   48

Festive   60

The Cookie Recipes   78

The Ice Cream Recipes   110

Refreshing Treats   116

Index   124

Acknowledgements   126

About the Author   128

INTRODUCTION

Cool, creamy vanilla ice cream surrounded by chewy chocolatey brownie. Crunchy, buttery oatmeal cookies encasing refreshing mint choc-chip ice cream, indulgently dipped in slightly bitter chocolate. Ice cream sandwiches are among the sweetest memories of my childhood ... just as much a part of summers growing up in California as running through the garden sprinklers in our swimsuits.

Ice cream sandwiches are traditionally made by 'sandwiching' ice cream between two baked cookies, biscuits or wafers. Combining the crunchy, chewy cookies with creamy, cold ice cream somehow more than doubles the resulting pleasure.

No wonder ice cream sandwiches for generations in the US have been a favourite treat for children and adults alike. They made their debut in New York City in the 1890s, and quickly caught on across the US, with one particular version being honoured as 'The Official Food of San Francisco'. They eventually found their way to places as diverse as Australia, Scotland and Singapore, where they are usually made by adding a scoop of ice cream between two layers of rainbow-coloured bread!

I launched my Buttercup Cake Shop in London in 2006. As we expanded into a premiere cupcake company with locations in Kent and London (including the 2012 Olympics site), we started to get quite a few enquiries about whether we also sold ice cream. This got me thinking – what goes better with cake than ice cream!? We began offering cupcakes blended with vanilla ice cream and called it a cupshake; ice cream on top of cupcakes ('cupcake sundae'); and my childhood favourite ... ice cream sandwiches.

Ice cream sandwiches made their UK debut at Buttercup in spring 2011 and have proven instantly popular. We bake the cookies fresh every day and assemble the sandwiches to order on the spot, so they are soft and ready to enjoy immediately. While initially I envisioned them being mostly popular with children, it turns out I wasn't the only adult keen to indulge! I especially get a kick out of watching stylish men in their twenties and thirties tuck in unreservedly. Today, ice cream sandwiches have become hotter than ever! They are the latest comfort food to receive gourmet status with bakeries and gelato shops in New York City, where endless possible combinations of ice cream and 'cookie' are available.

In this book you will discover easy, step-by-step instructions on how to prepare, assemble and decorate delicious and novel sandwiches. Rose Meringues are ideal for a dinner party, and White Chocolate Chip Teddies will be a hit at any child's birthday. In addition, try our special treats for seasonal celebrations, such as Graveyard Coffins for Halloween and Flocked Trees for Christmas. And when nothing but the most indulgent treat will suffice, try our Caramel Snickerdoodle-doos – an irresistible combination of vanilla, caramel and cinnamon – or Aloha Sandwiches – a marriage of chocolate, toasted coconut and macadamia nut that will transport you to paradise!

Whichever the occasion, you'll find that making ice cream sandwiches is straightforward. It's an activity that can be shared with children, and with some adult help, cutting and filling the sandwiches is not only a doddle but also boosts their confidence in the kitchen.

For ease of use, the recipes are divided into three sections: the sandwiches (with assembly and decoration ideas), cookie recipes and main ice cream recipes. We have included recipes for ice cream you can make at home, including some that don't require an ice-cream maker and still result in a creamy, smooth texture. The division of cookie and ice cream recipes also makes mixing and matching easier should you want to customise. Feel free to experiment with flavour combinations, add your own decorations and adjust the portion sizes as you wish.

If you are short on time, there is always the option of using store-bought cookies and/or ice cream. You can easily make any of the cookies or ice creams a day ahead and do the assembly and decoration separately. Ice cream sandwiches can be stored in the freezer for several weeks, so they're the perfect solution to impromptu get-togethers with friends, last-minute playdates or when you crave a guilty pleasure.

I hope you will have fun in the kitchen with the recipes that follow and wish you pleasurable satisfaction with the resulting creations. Happy Sandwiching!

COOKS' NOTES

Equipment

For all recipes requiring an ice-cream maker, I use a simple 1.1 litre (2 pint) capacity model, where the 'bowl' portion is popped into the freezer for at least several hours before adding ingredients and churning. With this type of machine, remember that the base must be fully re-frozen between each batch.

Speciality ice cream sandwich moulds by Tovolo or Kitchen Craft can be used for creating shapes and assembling, including making an 'imprint' on the top of the sandwich. Wilton now sells a pour- or scoop-in sandwich mould that can be used for round brownie or cookie bases. Otherwise, standard cookie cutters may be used.

Baking times vary with different oven and tin types. For the brownies and bars, I use tins from Lakeland, which measure approximately 38 x 25 x 2cm (15 x 10 x 1in). For the cookie recipes, I use insulated cookie sheets. The recipes give conventional oven temperatures. However, I use a fan oven, which requires a lower oven temperature and often shorter cooking times. In many recipes, a range of cooking times is given to allow for potential adjustments.

Ingredients

Throughout the book, for convenience I have given two sets of measures – metric (UK) and imperial (US). The latter is found in brackets. Always stick to one system throughout a recipe – never mix the two. 'Cups' refer to the standard measuring cup, and for flour I have used the 'dip and sweep' method of filling the cup, giving a generous measure. UK weight measures have been rounded for convenience.

I've used large eggs in all cases, and the butter is unsalted. Creams vary by recipe. Using double cream will render thicker, more decadent results, versus whipping cream, which gives an airier ice cream.

DECADENT

Whether it's toasted nuts, creamy caramel, chocolate mousse or several of these combined, sometimes nothing but the most wickedly indulgent treat will do. When you have one of those occasions, this is the chapter for you! Here you can choose from sandwich options such as Chocolate Hazelnut – a light but rich combination of brownie, fluffy chocolate and hazelnuts; Butterscotchies – a sweet punch of chewy butterscotch brownie with custardy vanilla ice cream and homemade butterscotch sauce; as well as Caramel Snickerdoodle-doos – an innocent-enough name for a heady combination of cinnamon, vanilla and caramel.

CARAMEL SNICKERDOODLE-DOO

My mother would often treat us kids to a Saturday trip to the beach, and we always pestered her on the way home to stop by Marianne's, famous for its 50+ flavours of home-made ice cream. The cinnamon caramel ice cream remains to this day one of my favourites in the world. The same flavour combination is probably what makes this recipe so comforting and irresistible. Reassuringly, Marianne's can still be found in its original spot on Ocean Street in Santa Cruz, California, but for those too far away, give this recipe a try!

Makes 6 sandwiches

12 Snickerdoodle Cookies (see p. 85)
1 batch of Vanilla Ice Cream (see p. 112) or 500ml (1 pint) premium store-bought

For the butterscotch sauce
110g (⅓ cup) light corn syrup or light golden syrup
135g (½ cup + 2 tbsp) soft light brown sugar, firmly packed
30g (2 tbsp) butter
⅛ tsp salt (about 3 pinches)
80ml (⅓ cup) double cream

1. To make the sauce, put the syrup, sugar, butter and salt in a medium, heavy-based saucepan and stir over a medium heat. Bring to the boil and keep stirring until the mixture is the consistency of a thick syrup, then remove from the heat. Allow to cool for 10 minutes, then mix in the double cream.
2. Make the Vanilla Ice Cream (see p. 112). Remove the canister from the ice-cream maker and drizzle butterscotch sauce over the soft ice cream, using a rubber spatula to marble it through before decanting into an airtight plastic storage container. (If using store-bought ice cream, take out of the freezer to soften for 3–4 minutes only, before marbling the butterscotch.) Freeze for at least 1 hour.
3. Make the Snickerdoodle Cookies as per the method on p. 85 and match up into similar-sized pairs. Scoop your desired amount of ice cream into the centre of the flat side of one cookie. Using an angled spatula, spread it evenly to within 1cm (½in) of the cookie edge. Place the matching cookie on top, flat-side down, and gently press just until the ice cream comes to the edge.
4. Serve immediately or place in a clean, airtight plastic container and return to the freezer. Cookies may be stacked but should not touch edges. If re-freezing, allow to sit at room temperature for about 3 minutes before enjoying.

PEANUT BUTTER DREAM

Those who like peanut butter won't be able to resist this combination of chocolate brownie sandwiched with fluffy peanut butter filling, adapted from a beloved recipe for peanut butter pie. This filling lends itself well to being sandwiched before freezing, and the sandwiches have the added benefit of holding their shape without melting.

Makes 6 sandwiches

12 Chewy Chocolate Brownies (see p. 82)
140ml (½ cup + 1 tbsp) whipping cream
110g (4oz) cream cheese
90g (½ cup) smooth peanut butter, without chunks or skins
100g (½ cup) granulated white sugar
10g (2 tsp) butter, softened
1 tsp pure vanilla extract

1. Cook the brownie base as instructed on p. 82, remembering to cut it as soon as it's out of the oven. Whilst this is cooking, whip the cream in a small bowl until fluffy, and set aside in the refrigerator or another cool place.
2. In a separate medium-sized bowl, beat the cream cheese, peanut butter, sugar, butter and vanilla until smooth. Fold the whipped cream into the peanut butter mixture until no streaks remain.
3. Once the brownies are completely cool, spread your desired amount of filling onto one brownie, on the side that was touching the tin, to about 5mm (¼ in) from the edges. Add a second brownie, tin-side down, and gently press for an even distribution until the filling reaches the edges. Repeat with the rest of the brownies. Store in airtight plastic containers and freeze for at least 2 hours before serving.

ALOHA SANDWICHES

This recipe is inspired by many summers enjoyed in the Hawaiian sun on the island of Maui, where, among other treats, they are renowned for Hula Pie, a concoction of coffee and chocolate ice cream over a chocolate crumb base, smothered in fudge sauce and macadamia nuts.

Makes 4 large or 8 small sandwiches

1 batch of All-American Chocolate Chip Cookie dough (see p. 88, and
    note instructions below)
40g (½ cup) coconut, toasted
60g (½ cup) macadamia nuts, lightly toasted and chopped
1 batch of Chocolate or Mocha Ice Cream (see p. 112 or 114) or 500ml (1 pint)
    store-bought, semi-softened

1. Bake the All-American Chocolate Chip Cookies as directed on p. 88. While still warm from the oven, cut into 8 large or 16 small rectangles. Allow to cool for at least 10 minutes before removing from the tin.
2. Spread the coconut on a flat plate and the chopped nuts on another. Once the cookies are completely cool, spoon some semi-softened ice cream onto one cookie, on the side that was touching the tin. Smooth down with an angled spatula, keeping an even distribution, until the ice cream is within 5mm (¼ in) of the edges. Add the second cookie, tin-side down. Gently and evenly press together until the ice cream reaches the edges.
3. Working quickly, roll the edges of the sandwich in the coconut then in the chopped nuts. Repeat with the rest of the cookies. Serve immediately or quickly store in an airtight plastic container (don't stack the cookies) and freeze.

BEVERLY HILLS DAHLINGS

Just like their namesake, these sandwiches manage to pay homage to healthy eating (thanks to the oatmeal) while being plenty rich and sporting their share of nuts! This recipe is best with home-made vanilla ice cream, but if you choose to substitute with a store-bought ice cream, do check the ingredients to ensure it's real dairy ice cream rather than an inferior product made from whey protein and vegetable oils.

Makes 9 sandwiches

18 Beverly Hills Cookies (see p. 98)
1 batch of Vanilla Ice Cream (see p. 112) or 500ml (1 pint) premium store-bought
90g (¾ cup) finely chopped toasted walnuts (optional)

1. Prepare the Beverly Hills Cookies as per the recipe on p. 98. Cool completely then match up equal-sized pairs.
2. Working with ice cream that has fully set in the freezer (i.e. not directly out of the ice-cream maker, when it will be too messy), use an angled spatula or dull knife to spread the desired amount onto the flat side of one cookie to within 5mm (¼ in) of the edges. Sprinkle with the chopped walnuts, if using.
3. Place the matching cookie on top, flat-side down, and gently press down until the ice cream reaches the edges. Serve immediately. Alternatively, place in an airtight plastic container and freeze until a few minutes before serving. The sandwiches may be stacked but avoid letting the edges touch.

MONKEY SANDWICHES

Monkeys love bananas and nuts, and so do kids … especially when combined with vanilla ice cream sandwiched between two brownies!

Makes 4 large or 8 small sandwiches

1 batch of Chewy Chocolate Brownie dough (see p. 82)
65g (½ cup) roasted peanuts, chopped
1 batch of Vanilla Ice Cream (see p. 112) or 500ml (1 pint) premium store-bought, semi-softened
2 fresh bananas, sliced

1. Bake the brownies as directed on p. 82. While still warm from the oven, cut into 8 large or 16 small rectangles. Allow to cool for at least 10 minutes before removing from the tin.
2. Spread the chopped peanuts on a plate. Once the brownies are completely cool, spoon the semi-softened ice cream onto one brownie, upside down. Smooth it down with an angled spatula, keeping an even distribution, until the ice cream is within 5mm (¼ in) from the edges.
3. Add the banana slices, then a second brownie, tin-side down. Gently and evenly press together until the ice cream reaches the edges. Working quickly, roll the edges of the sandwich in the chopped nuts. Repeat with the rest of the brownies.
4. Serve immediately or quickly store in an airtight plastic container (don't stack the sandwiches), and freeze. If frozen, allow to sit for 3 minutes before serving.

BUTTERSCOTCHIES

This is for when you are in the mood for something chewy and sweet! You can make the butterscotch sauce ahead and store it in the refrigerator.

Makes 4 large or 6 medium sandwiches

8 large or 12 medium Butterscotch Brownies (see p. 84)
1 batch of Butterscotch Sauce (see p. 12)
1 batch of Vanilla Ice Cream (see p. 112) or 500ml (1 pint) premium store-bought

1. Due to the butterscotch sauce, it is best to assemble these right before serving. If you prefer to make them ahead, have ready a couple of airtight plastic containers, kept cold in the freezer.
2. Make the Butterscotch Brownies as per the recipe on p. 84 and cut into shapes while still warm from the oven. Allow to cool before removing from the tin. Match into similar-sized pairs.
3. Ensure the butterscotch sauce has cooled to room temperature before assembling the sandwiches, to avoid melting the ice cream. Working with ice cream that has fully set in the freezer (i.e. not directly out of the ice-cream maker, when it will be too messy), use an angled spatula or dull knife to spread the desired amount onto the flat side of one brownie to within 5mm (¼ in) of the edges.
4. Make a small well shape in the centre of the ice cream and spoon 1–2 teaspoons of butterscotch sauce into the well. Work with cooled sauce if possible; however, if it is proving too difficult to scoop, warm it up in the microwave for just 5 seconds or warm gently in a heatproof bowl set over a pan of hot (not boiling) water.
5. Place the matching brownie on top, flat-side down, and very gently press down until the ice cream reaches the edges. Serve immediately if possible. Otherwise, pop the sandwiches into your cold plastic containers without stacking (to avoid the butter-scotch running over the outside of the brownie.) If re-frozen, let sit for 3 minutes before serving.

BOUNTY BITES

Somehow the pleasure of chewy coconut cookies and chocolate ice cream, when combined, is more than the sum of their parts. These will retain their maximum chewiness and flavour if you fill them just before serving.

Makes 8 medium or 16 bite-sized sandwiches

16 medium or 32 bite-sized Coconut Macaroons (see p. 96, but note instruction below if adding cocoa)
2 tbsp cocoa powder (optional)
1 batch of Chocolate Ice Cream (see p. 112) or 500ml (1 pint) premium store-bought

1. Make the Coconut Macaroons as per the recipe on p. 96. If adding cocoa, first heat the sweetened condensed milk in a pan over a low heat, then whisk in the cocoa powder until well combined. Remove from the heat and use as directed.
2. Once the macaroons have baked and cooled, match them up into equal-sized pairs. Scoop your desired amount of ice cream onto the flat side of the first macaroon. Use an angled spatula or dull knife to spread the ice cream to within 5mm (¼ in) of the edges.
3. Gently press on the second macaroon, with the flat side against the ice cream. Serve immediately or store in the freezer in an airtight plastic container. If frozen, allow to sit for 3 minutes before serving.

CHOCOLATE HAZELNUT SANDWICHES

These are best made with my chocolate ice cream, which is made like a mousse using plain chocolate, so has a more decadent, less sugary effect than commercial chocolate ice creams. You can toast the hazelnuts for extra flavour and can also opt to add coffee liqueur when entertaining adult friends. This sandwich also works well with Tin Roof or Mocha Cookies (see p. 101 and 104).

Makes 6–8 sandwiches

1 batch of Chocolate Ice Cream (see p. 112)
60ml (¼ cup) coffee liqueur (optional)
50g (⅓ cup) hazelnuts, chopped
1 batch of Chewy Chocolate Brownie dough (see p. 82)

1. Make the Chocolate Ice Cream as described on p. 112 but when folding the chocolate into the whipped cream mixture also fold in the coffee liqueur (if using) and the hazelnuts. Freeze as directed.
2. Meanwhile make and bake the brownies (see p. 82). While still warm, cut into your desired shapes with a knife or cutter, remembering to cut shapes in pairs. If your cutter is not symmetrical, cut every other brownie with the opposite side of the cutter so that they will match up into sandwiches. Remove from the tin only once cooled.
3. When the brownies are completely cooled, spoon the ice cream onto the tin-side of one brownie. Use a small palette knife or dull knife to spread it to within 1cm (½in) of the edges. Place the matching shape on top, tin-side down, and press gently, without allowing the filling to spill out.
4. Place the sandwiches in an airtight plastic container. If you need to stack them, place sheets of greaseproof paper (waxed paper) between the layers. Freeze until ready to serve. Allow to sit at room temperature for 3 minutes before serving.

MOCHA MORSELS

This recipe, combining two of my favourite flavours – coffee and chocolate – is sure to please even your more sophisticated guests. For a richer flavour, you can sprinkle a layer of cocoa powder over the ice cream before adding the top cookie.

Makes 6 sandwiches

12 Mocha Cookies (see p. 104)
1 batch of Mocha Ice Cream (see p. 114)

1. Make the Mocha Cookies as per the recipe on p. 104 and leave to cool. Follow the recipe for Mocha Ice Cream (see p. 114) but don't freeze it.
2. Once the cookies are fully cooled, match them up into similar-sized pairs. Spread a 2cm (¾in) layer of filling onto one cookie, on the side that was touching the cookie sheet. Smooth the edges with an angled spatula or smooth-edged knife. Place the second cookie, flat-side down, onto the filling.
3. Place the sandwiches carefully in an airtight plastic container. If you need to stack them, place sheets of greaseproof paper (waxed paper) between the layers. Freeze for at least 1½ hours before serving.

BANOFFEE SANDWICHES

The banoffee cupcakes at Buttercup are the favourite choice among our male customers, so that was the inspiration behind this recipe, which combines fresh banana bread with vanilla ice cream and butterscotch sauce.

Makes 6 sandwiches

1 batch of Vanilla Ice Cream (see p. 112) or 500ml (1 pint) premium store-bought
1 batch of Butterscotch Sauce (see p. 12)
1 loaf or 6 mini loaves of Banana Bread (see p. 106)
8 tbsp (½ cup) butterscotch or white chocolate curls or chips (optional)

1. Make the Vanilla Ice Cream (see p. 112), then remove the canister from the ice-cream maker. (If using store-bought, remove from the freezer to soften for 3–4 minutes only, or microwave on 80 per cent power for 10–15 seconds). Drizzle the butterscotch sauce over the soft ice cream, using a rubber spatula to marble it through. Decant into an airtight plastic container and freeze for at least 1 hour.
2. Use this time to make the Banana Bread as directed in the recipe on p. 106. Once cooled, slice the loaf into six slices of your desired thickness, then cut each slice in half from top to bottom. If using mini loaves, slice each loaf lengthwise.
3. Scoop your desired amount of ice cream into the centre of the cut side of one slice. Using an angled spatula, spread it evenly to within 1cm (½in) of the edges. Place the matching slice of banana bread on top, cut-side down, and gently press just until the ice cream comes to the edges. If using, place the curls or chips on a flat plate and roll the edges of the sandwiches in them.
4. These should ideally be served immediately. If you cannot serve right away, place in an airtight plastic container (the sandwiches can be stacked) and return to the freezer. Once frozen, allow to sit for a couple of minutes at room temperature before serving.

GINGER LEMON GEMS

Ginger-lovers will especially appreciate its pairing with my zesty lemon ice cream. The intense flavours make the smaller-sized gems a perfect accompaniment to a light afternoon tea. When making the ice cream, ensure you use real dairy cream. UHT (long-life) creams will work but avoid dairy substitutes, which are made mostly with oil.

Makes 12 small sandwich 'gems'

1 batch of Lemon Ice Cream (see p. 115)
1 batch of Soft Ginger Cookie dough (see p. 92)

1. Follow the recipe for the Soft Ginger Cookies (see p. 92) and drop 24 balls of the mixture onto the cookie sheet from a spring-action melon baller (or arrange heaped teaspoons). Reduce the baking time to 4–6 minutes.
2. Once the cookies have completely cooled, spoon some of the lemon ice cream onto the flat side of one cookie (the side that was touching the cookie sheet), and gently place the second cookie on top, flat-side down, pressing only enough to adhere to the cream.
3. Place the sandwiches – without stacking – in an airtight plastic container and freeze for at least 1 hour. Take out of the freezer immediately before serving.

FRESH 'N' FRUITY

While commercially available ice cream
sandwiches nearly always include a
combination of vanilla and chocolate,
for some occasions you may prefer
something lighter, fresh and fruity.
On the following pages you will find a
plethora of options, including the very
light Lemon Creams and Melon Sorbet
Butterflies, and a creamy, custardy fresh
fig ice cream spread between two Rolled
Vanilla Cookies. One of my favourites
here is the tangy Mascarpone Ice Cream
sandwiched between soft and spicy
Pumpkin Spice Cookies, which provide
a nice fruit flavour while making a
satisfying pudding ... perfect to complete
an autumn-themed meal.

APPLE PIE A LA MODE

A satisfying treat at any time of year but especially welcome in the autumn when apples are plentiful.

Makes 9 sandwiches

18 Grated Apple Cookies (see p. 91)
1 batch of Vanilla Ice Cream (see p. 112) or 500ml (1 pint) premium store-bought

1. Prepare the Grated Apple Cookies as per the recipe on p. 91. Allow them to cool completely then match up equal-sized pairs.
2. Scoop the desired amount of ice cream onto the flat side of the first cookie. Use an angled spatula or dull knife to spread the ice cream to within 5mm (¼ in) of the edges. Gently press on the second cookie, flat-side down, until the ice cream reaches the edges. Neaten up the sides with an angled spatula if desired.
3. Serve immediately or store in the freezer in an airtight plastic container. If frozen, allow to sit for 3 minutes before serving.

PEACHES 'N' CREAM

Peaches epitomise summer and make an ice cream that is both refreshing and indulgent. When paired with a classic Rolled Vanilla Cookie, the result is sumptuous! You can substitute nectarines for peaches but ensure either is perfectly ripe.

Makes 8 or more sandwiches

1 batch of Rolled Vanilla Cookie dough (see p. 80)
4 egg yolks
¼ tsp salt
150g (¾ cup) granulated white sugar
570ml (2¼ cups + 2 tbsp) double cream
90ml (¼ cup + 2 tbsp) milk
500g (2½ cups) mashed peaches (7–8, depending on size)

1. Prepare and cook the Rolled Vanilla Cookie dough as per the recipe on p. 80, cutting into your desired shapes. If you are using a sandwich mould or cookie cutter with a pattern, use while the cookies are still hot from the oven, carefully pressing down the mould/cutter to imprint the pattern onto half of the cookies. Cool completely then match up into equal-shaped pairs.
2. Beat the egg yolks in a blender or with an electric mixer until thick. Add the salt and blend in the sugar in three parts. Scald 90ml (¼ cup + 2 tbsp) of the cream with all the milk in a heatproof bowl over a pan of simmering water.
3. Pour a small amount of the milk mixture into the egg yolk mixture. Then add all the yolk mixture to the milk mixture and cook, stirring constantly over simmering water until the mixture forms a thick custard (coating the back of a spoon). Remove from the heat and leave to cool.
4. Mix the mashed fruit with the remaining 480ml (2 cups) of cream, add the custard mixture and refrigerate until cold. Pour into an ice-cream maker and follow the manufacturer's instructions. Freeze for at least a further 2 hours before using as a filling.
5. If you used a sandwich mould or tall cutter, re-fit the first cookie upside down in the base of the mould or under the cutter. Place the body of the mould over as a guide for adding ice cream and fill to your desired thickness. Remove the mould or cutter and gently place the top cookie right-side up on top of the ice cream.
6. Serve immediately or place in an airtight plastic container. Cookies may be stacked but you should avoid their edges touching.

FRESH FIG (PIG) SANDWICHES

The combination of rich custard and fresh figs makes a delightful indulgent filling, and combined with vanilla cookies, it makes a lovely end-of-summer treat.

Makes 12 sandwiches

1 batch of Rolled Vanilla Cookie dough (see p. 80)
4 eggs
200g (1 cup) granulated white sugar
480ml (2 cups) milk
480ml (2 cups) double or whipping cream
1½ tsp pure vanilla extract
¼ tsp salt
¼ tsp nutmeg
4 fresh figs, peeled and mashed

1. Make the Rolled Vanilla Cookie dough (see p. 80). While the dough is refrigerating, make the ice cream, as follows.
2. Beat the eggs in a blender until thick or use an electric mixer. Blend in the sugar in three parts. Combine with the milk and cream in a heatproof bowl, put over a pan of simmering, but not boiling, water (or in a double boiler) and cook, stirring constantly, until it becomes a thick custard.
3. Remove from the heat and add the vanilla extract, salt and nutmeg. Fold in the mashed figs. Refrigerate until cool then pour into an ice-cream maker and follow the manufacturer's instructions. Freeze for at least a further 2 hours before filling.
4. Use this freezing time to bake the cookie dough as directed on p. 80. Use a shaped cutter or a knife to cut out 24 cookies. If you are making imprints on the top of your cookie, do this to half of them while they are still hot and before removing from the cookie sheet. Once the cookies are fully cooled, match them up into pairs.
5. If using a mould, place one cookie into the mould, the side that was touching the cookie sheet facing up. Add ice cream, using the mould to guide its shape. Push down gently with the plunger to distribute the ice cream evenly into shape. Remove the mould, then place a second cookie, sheet-side down, on top of the ice cream.
6. If *not* using a mould, take an angled spatula and spread ice cream evenly to within 5mm (¼ in) of the edges. Place another cookie on top, sheet-side down, and gently press until the ice cream comes to the edges. Serve immediately or freeze in airtight plastic containers (they can be stacked). If frozen, allow to sit for 3 minutes before serving.

ELDERFLOWER AMARETTOS

Elderflower is a quintessentially English flavour that I only discovered once I'd lived here for a few years. It's now one of my favourite flavours. My neighbour Catriona showed me how simple it is to make a syrup for cordials, and I found that it easily adjusted for this sorbet, too.

Pick elderflower heads that are growing away from the roadside, where they might be dusty and reach for the higher limbs as those are the cleanest. Find buds that are open but have not yet started to wilt. Ensure you are collecting elderflower and not a lookalike by checking against photos (available online) and of course use your nose to confirm the trademark sweet scent.

Makes 6–8 sorbet sandwiches

700g (3½ cups) caster sugar (superfine granulated)
2 lemons, grated zest and juice
10 elderflower heads
12–16 Amaretto Biscuits (see p. 99)

1. First make the sugar syrup by placing the sugar and 1 litre (4¼ cups) water in a large saucepan over a moderate heat. Stir constantly until the sugar has dissolved. Then increase the heat just until the mixture boils. Reduce slightly to a steady simmer until thickened (about 5 minutes).
2. Remove from the heat and add the lemon zest and elderflower heads. Cool then strain to remove the flowers. Add the lemon juice and refrigerate until cold. While waiting, make the Amaretto Biscuits as per the recipe on p. 90.
3. Put the cold sorbet mixture into an ice-cream maker and follow the manufacturer's instructions. Transfer to an airtight plastic container, allowing at least 1cm (½in) of empty space at the top of the container. Allow to freeze for at least 1½ hours.
4. Match up equal-sized biscuits and ensure they are fully cooled. Apply a scoop of sorbet to the middle of the flat side of one of the biscuits. Flatten with an angled spatula or dull knife. Then use the flat size of the other biscuit to gently press down until the sorbet nearly reaches the edges. It's best to serve immediately as these cookies can become brittle when frozen.

LEMON CREAMS

The combination of a very light texture and the citrussy zest makes this cream a perfect complement for soft oatmeal cookies. The resulting ice cream sandwich will appeal to children and adults alike and makes a nice surprise to end a family meal. The filling can be made a day or two ahead and should be soft enough to scoop directly from the container and spread onto cookies.

Makes 6 large or 8 medium sandwiches

12 large or 16 medium Soft Oatmeal Cookies (see p. 89)
1 batch of Lemon Ice Cream (see p. 115)

1. Make the Soft Oatmeal Cookies as described on p. 89. Cool completely and match similar sizes into pairs.
2. Spoon some of the ice cream onto the flat side of one cookie (the side that was touching the cookie sheet), and spread to within 1cm (½in) of the edge. Place the matching cookie on top, flat-side down, and gently press until the filling approaches the edges. Clean up any over-spill with the back of a small palette knife or dull knife.
3. Serve immediately or put in an airtight plastic container (they can be stacked) and store in the freezer.

BANANA SPLIT SANDWICHES

Inspired by a classic ice-cream parlour favourite, these combine the tastes of fresh banana, chocolate ice cream, marshmallows and toasted nuts.

Makes 6 sandwiches

1 loaf or 6 mini loaves of Banana Bread (see p. 106)
100g (2 cups) miniature marshmallows
200g (1¼ cups) milk chocolate chips
120ml (½ cup) single cream ('half & half')
240ml (1 cup) double or whipping cream
40g (⅓ cup) chopped toasted pecans or walnuts

1. Prepare the Banana Bread as per the recipe on p. 106 and allow to cool fully.
2. In a medium saucepan over a low heat, combine all but 25g (½ cup) of the marshmallows, the chocolate chips and single cream. Stir until the chocolate is melted and the mixture is smooth. Remove from the heat and cool completely.
3. Whip the cream and set aside, away from the heat, until the chocolate mixture has completely cooled, then fold the whipped cream into the chocolate, along with the remaining marshmallows and the nuts.
4. Cut the Banana Bread into slices about 1.5cm (½in) thick. If you opted for the full-sized loaf, cut each slice in half to form two rectangles. If you made mini loaves, slice each one lengthwise.
5. Scoop the desired amount of filling onto one slice and use a dull knife or angled spatula to spread it across the bread. Place the matching slice on top, and gently press until the filling comes to the edges. Repeat with the rest. Freeze until set, for about 1 hour, then serve.

ROSE MERINGUES

While working in Los Angeles, a Persian colleague initiated me in the delights of rose ice cream. I've been unsuccessful in re-discovering the little specialist shop she showed me in an unfamiliar part of town and indeed haven't found any rose ice cream in London despite the many specialist shops; however, I have been delighted with the results of this recipe, which I adapted to recreate the light, fluffy texture and unique flavour that I fell in love with years ago. It's particularly heavenly when served between two Vanilla Meringue Cookies. You can find rose syrup in specialist Persian or Indian grocers or sometimes in the international section of a large supermarket. If struggling, substitute 2 teaspoons of rosewater and increase the food colouring by a few extra drops.

Makes 8 sandwiches

16 Vanilla Meringues (see p. 86)
480ml (2 cups) single cream ('half & half')
360ml (1½ cups) double cream
120ml (½ cup) milk
100g (½ cup) granulated white sugar
4 tsp rose syrup
Pinch of salt
2–3 drops of red food colouring

1. Prepare the Vanilla Meringues as per the recipe on p. 86. They look especially nice with coloured sugar strands or hundreds and thousands sprinkled on top prior to baking. You can co-ordinate the timing so that they are drying in the oven and cooling while your rose ice cream is hardening in the freezer.
2. Ensure all the dairy ingredients are cold. In a medium or large bowl with an electric mixer, whisk together all the ingredients for 1–2 minutes, until the sugar is dissolved. Pour into an ice-cream maker and follow the manufacturer's instructions.
3. Transfer to an airtight plastic container, allowing at least 1cm (½in) of empty space at the top of the container as the mixture will expand as it freezes. Allow to freeze for at least 2 hours.
4. Match the cooled meringues into pairs of similar sizes. Scoop some rose ice cream onto the flat side of one meringue and gently spread to within 1cm (½in) of the edge. Place the matching meringue on top, flat-side down, and very gently press until the ice cream reaches the edges. Serve immediately.

MELON SORBET BUTTERFLIES

These melon sorbet sandwiches are just like biting into the ripe fruit itself – sweet and cold. Perfect to top off your next outdoor get-together!

Makes 6 sandwiches

1 batch of Rolled Vanilla Cookie dough (see p. 80)
1 medium-sized ripe honeydew melon, seeded, peeled and cubed
3 tbsp fresh lemon juice (about 1–1½ lemons)
250g (1¼ cups) caster sugar (superfine granulated)
Pinch of black pepper

1. Prepare the cookie dough as per the recipe on p. 80, and while it is refrigerating, you can prepare the sorbet.
2. Use a food processor to blitz the melon into a purée. Add the other ingredients and process for another 45 seconds. Decant into an airtight plastic container and refrigerate until very cold.
3. Transfer to an ice-cream maker and follow the manufacturer's instructions. Replace in the airtight plastic container and freeze for at least 2 hours before using to fill your sandwiches. The sorbet should remain easy to scoop even after freezing for longer.
4. Meanwhile, finish making and baking your cookies. Roll out the cookie dough and cut out at least 12 butterflies using a sandwich mould or shaped cookie cutter. It is wise to cut out one or two extra in case of mishaps. Bake as instructed.
5. If you are using a sandwich mould, gently stamp the pattern on half of the cookies immediately after taking them out of the oven. If not using a mould, you can create your own pattern on the wings by using the handle of a decoratively patterned spoon, the back of a miniature espresso or mustard spoon, the tines of a fork or other kitchen implements. Take care not to press too hard.
6. Once sufficiently frozen, scoop the desired amount of sorbet onto the underneath side of a non-decorated butterfly, distributing evenly. Use the mould or cutter placed over the cookie as a guide for adding the sorbet. Remove the mould and gently place a decorated cookie on top, with the decorated side facing up. If using a sandwich mould, you can use the plunger. Serve immediately or quickly place in an airtight plastic container (they can be stacked) and freeze.

MARMALADE MADELEINES

These are the perfect light refreshment for when hosting 'coffee mornings'. Their zesty flavour combines particularly well with Earl Grey tea, and the filling stays neatly where it belongs even if allowed to thaw a bit. Store-bought madeleines will work fine at a pinch, and I've found any spare filling is right at home atop an oaty biscuit!

Makes 16 small sandwiches (allow 2–3 per serving)

16 Zesty Madeleines (see p. 105)
1 batch of Marmalade Ice Cream (see p. 115)

1. Make the Zesty Madeleines as per the recipe on p. 105 and allow to cool fully.
2. Make the Marmalade Ice Cream as described on p. 115 but don't freeze it.
3. Using a knife with a serrated blade, carefully slice each madeleine lengthwise using a gentle sawing motion. Cover one side with a generous tablespoonful of the ice cream. Spread to the edges, then place the other half on top.
4. Put in an airtight plastic container – without stacking – and freeze for at least 1½ hours. The unfrozen ice cream mixture also keeps nicely in the fridge for a day or two (well covered) if you want to make it ahead to fill and freeze on a subsequent day.

PUMPKIN MASCARPONE SANDWICHES

The tangy taste of mascarpone ice cream makes a tasty contrast to the warm, spicy chocolate flavour and chewy texture of my Pumpkin Spice Cookies. Together they make an excellent treat for an autumn day, regardless of the weather! Low-fat cream cheese may be substituted for the fromage frais.

Makes 6 large or 8 medium sandwiches

12 large or 16 medium Pumpkin Spice Cookies (see p. 95)
1 batch of Mascarpone Ice Cream (see p. 114)

1. Make the Pumpkin Spice Cookies as per the recipe on p. 95 and allow to cool completely.
2. Match up the cooled cookies into pairs of similar sizes. Scoop the ice cream onto the flat side of one cookie and gently spread to within 1cm (½in) of the edges. Place the matching cookie on top, flat-side down, and very gently press until the ice cream reaches the edges.
3. Serve immediately or quickly place in an airtight plastic container in the freezer until ready to serve. If you need to stack them, place sheets of greaseproof paper (waxed paper) between the layers.

KIDELICIOUS

While not every child is the same, I've found that the smaller customers at our shops tend to divide into those who like the simpler offerings, such as vanilla and chocolate, as plain as can be, and those who like the other extreme. This chapter is for the latter! So if your kids can't get enough of sweet chocolate chips, marshmallows or candy toppings, you'll be sure to find something to elicit a 'wow!' from them. And of course, the recipes in this section will likewise delight those of us who haven't grown out of appreciating that 'more' sometimes *is* more. When you're up for one of these recipes, you might want to keep the main dish on the lighter side to leave plenty of room for dessert!

CHOCOLATE MARSHMALLOW BROWNIES

If ever there was a recipe to please children, this is it! You can add roasted peanuts for nut-lovers, including adult chocoholics. This recipe is especially quick and simple to prepare and doesn't require an ice-cream maker, so it's great for when you are short on time.

Makes 4 large or 6 medium sandwiches

8 large or 12 medium Chewy Chocolate Brownies (see p. 82)
100g (2 cups) miniature marshmallows
200g (1¼ cups) milk chocolate chips
120ml (½ cup) single cream ('half & half')
240ml (1 cup) double or whipping cream
40g (⅓ cup) roasted peanuts, chopped (optional)

1. Prepare the brownies as per the recipe on p. 82. While still warm, cut into rectangles or other desired shapes, ensuring to make pairs of the same size. Set aside to cool completely.
2. In a medium saucepan over a low heat, combine all but 25g (½ cup) of the marshmallows, the chocolate chips and single cream. Stir until the chocolate is melted and the mixture is smooth. Remove from the heat and cool completely.
3. Whip the double or whipping cream and set aside, away from the heat, until the chocolate mixture has completely cooled, then fold the whipped cream into the chocolate mixture, along with the remaining marshmallows and nuts.
4. Fill the brownie sandwiches, ensuring the cream is applied to the flat sides that were touching the bottom of the tin. If cut into decorative shapes, use the same cutter again to guide the filling into the proper shape. Store in an airtight plastic container and freeze until firm, for at least 1 hour.

WHITE CHOCOLATE CHIP TEDDIES

These are decadent – kids, and 'kids-at-heart', will love 'em! The combination of chocolate-chip cookie and rich vanilla ice cream makes them perfect for a birthday party or other special celebration. If you are short on time, the cookie recipe lends itself well to a wide variety of store-bought ice cream flavours, particularly vanilla or chocolate. And if you prefer a less sweet version, you can swap in plain (semi-sweet) chocolate chips for the white ones.

Makes 6 medium sandwiches

640ml (2⅔ cups) whipping or double cream, divided
100g (½ cup) granulated white sugar
Pinch of salt
⅓ vanilla pod (optional)
1 tsp pure vanilla extract
1 batch of White Chocolate Chip Cookie dough (see p. 93)

1. In a small saucepan over a low heat, scald, but do not boil, 160ml (⅔ cup) of the cream.
2. Remove from the heat and vigorously stir in the sugar and salt until dissolved. If using the vanilla pod, add now and leave to soak. Allow to cool to room temperature, then remove the vanilla pod, scrape the seeds into the mixture and discard the pod. Chill in the refrigerator.
3. Once cold, add the remaining cream and the vanilla extract and stir. Put in an ice-cream maker, and follow the manufacturer's instructions. When ready, decant into an airtight plastic container and freeze for at least 1½ hours.
4. Meanwhile, follow the recipe for the White Chocolate Chip Cookies (see p. 93), using a 38 x 25 x 2cm (15 x 10 x 1in) baking tin. After baking and while still quite warm, use a teddy-bear shaped cookie cutter to cut out 12 teddy shapes, cutting one right next to the other but avoiding the very edges of the tin, which tend to be crunchier. After cutting all of them, carefully remove from the tin once still slightly warm and allow to cool on a rack.
5. Once completely cool, replace the cutter over one cookie. Cover with some of the ice cream, using an angled spatula to ensure it spreads across the entire shape. Remove the cutter and cover the ice cream with a second cookie, tin-side down. Press very gently just until it adheres.
6. Repeat with the rest and serve immediately or place carefully in airtight plastic containers. If you must stack sandwiches, use greaseproof paper between layers.

S'MORE SANDWICHES

I first discovered s'mores as a child, while staying at a friend's family cabin in the California Redwood Forest. They're a delicious treat, traditionally made over a campfire, and part of the fun is in taking your time to roast the marshmallow evenly. While this recipe has all your favourite ingredients for the real thing, you won't need a campfire to enjoy these! If you can't find mini marshmallows, regular-sized ones can be cut into four pieces so that the assembled sandwiches are still thin enough to eat comfortably.

Makes 6 medium sandwiches

1 batch of Chewy Chocolate Brownie dough (see p. 82)
7–8 digestive biscuits or graham cracker halves
1 batch of Chocolate Ice Cream (see p. 112) or 500ml (1 pint) premium store-bought
30g (¾ cup) mini marshmallows

1. Preheat the oven to 180°C (350°F), Gas Mark 4. Spread the brownie dough into the tin as described in the recipe on p. 82.
2. Before popping into the oven, break up the digestive biscuits into 8–10 pieces each and divide evenly over the batter. Gently push into the batter slightly so that they will remain attached once baked. Bake as directed.
3. While still warm from the oven, cut the brownies into 12 even rectangles. Leave to cool for at least 10 minutes before removing from the tin.
4. Allow the ice cream to soften, then spoon one-sixth of the ice cream onto the underside of one brownie. Spread evenly until it's about 5mm (¼ in) from the edges. Place 10–12 mini marshmallows on top. Add the second brownie, tin-side down, and gently press until the ice cream comes to the edges. Serve immediately or freeze in an airtight plastic container. If you need to stack sandwiches, place sheets of greaseproof paper (waxed paper) between the layers.

PEANUT BUTTER BITES

For a classic American combination of flavours, nothing beats peanut butter and chocolate. These are especially decadent due to the chocolate chips in the cookies themselves, so we recommend they be made small.

Makes 6 bite-sized sandwiches

1 batch of Tin Roof Cookie dough (see p. 101)
Butter, for greasing
Flour, for flattening
1 batch of Chocolate Ice Cream (see p. 112) or 500ml (1 pint) premium store-bought
8 tbsp (½ cup) chocolate vermicelli (sprinkles)

1. Prepare the Tin Roof Cookie dough (see p. 101). Grease a cookie sheet. Drop small, even amounts (about 1 level tablespoonful) approximately 7cm (3in) apart on the greased cookie sheet. Use the flat bottom of a glass (dipped each time in flour) to flatten to approximately 1cm (½in) high.
2. Bake as per the recipe on p. 101 just until the cookies are starting to turn golden on the edges, about 7–8 minutes. Cool completely on a wire rack.
3. If using my chocolate ice cream, make it as described on p. 112 but do not freeze it. Pair up similar-sized cookies, spread the desired amount of ice cream on the flat side of one cookie (the side that was touching the cookie sheet) and gently place the second cookie on top, flat-side down. Press until the filling reaches the edges.
4. Spread the vermicelli on a plate with edges. Gently roll the sides of the sandwiches in the vermicelli so that it sticks to the filling.
5. Store in an airtight plastic container. Cookies may be stacked but ensure they are not touching each other on the sides. If using store-bought ice cream, serve immediately. Otherwise freeze for at least 1½ hours before serving.

CHOCOLATE CANDY CRUSH

You may find that only the young will have the appetite to finish off this indulgent combination of cookie, ice cream and chocolate candy bar ... or you may be surprised! Either way, with the rich combination, I recommend making the cookies on the smaller side. Note that the chocolate will adhere much better if it is finely chopped and the ice cream is neither too soft nor rock hard.

Makes 6 sandwiches

12 Soft Oatmeal Cookies (see p. 89)
3 regular-sized chocolate candy bars, such as Snickers®, Mars®, Daim®
   (US: Heath®), etc., finely chopped or crushed
1 batch of Vanilla Ice Cream (see p. 112) or 500ml (1 pint) premium store-bought

1. Make the Soft Oatmeal Cookies as directed in the recipe on p. 89 and once they are fully cooled, match up similar-sized pairs. Finely chop the chocolate candy bars and set aside on a rimmed plate or shallow bowl.
2. Spread a 2cm (¾in) layer of firm ice cream onto the flat side of one cookie. Using an angled spatula, pat the ice cream down evenly until it nearly reaches the rim along the entire edge. Place a second cookie onto the filling, flat-side down, and gently push down until the ice cream starts to extend beyond the rim.
3. Quickly roll the rim, in a circle, through the chopped chocolate pieces until the edges of the sandwich are covered. While filling and rolling the remaining sandwiches, store those already made in the freezer, as they will melt more quickly with the chocolate coating.
4. Serve immediately or keep in an airtight plastic container in the freezer until ready to enjoy. If you need to stack them, place sheets of greaseproof paper (waxed paper) between the layers. If frozen, allow to sit for 3 minutes before serving.

MARMALADE BEAR SANDWICHES

Inspired by Paddington, the iconic bear from the children's tales who sure likes his marmalade sandwiches, you'll love these bear-shaped chocolate brownie sandwiches with marmalade ice cream filling! Note that kids tend to like them better if you call it 'orange ice cream' as some may have a prejudice against marmalade due to its texture.

Makes 6 medium sandwiches

1 batch of Chewy Chocolate Brownie dough (see p. 82)
1 batch of Marmalade Ice Cream (see p. 115)

1. Prepare the brownies as per the recipe on p. 82. While still warm, cut into shapes using a teddy-bear cookie cutter. Set aside to cool completely.
2. Make the Marmalade Ice Cream as per p. 115, but do not freeze.
3. Scoop the desired amount of unfrozen ice cream mixture onto the middle of one brownie, on the side that was touching the tin. With an angled spatula, gently spread the ice cream evenly outward towards the edges. (Use your clean cookie cutter over the brownie as a guide.) Wipe the back of the spatula before evening out the 'walls' of the ice cream. Gently place another brownie, tin-side down, on top.
4. Store in an airtight plastic container and freeze until firm, for at least 1 hour. If you need to stack the sandwiches, place sheets of greaseproof paper (waxed paper) between the layers.

FESTIVE

In this section you will find ideas to make special occasions stand out with themed ice cream sandwiches. Try Mint Chip Valentines for your loved ones in February or, for something unique at Halloween, take a crack at Graveyard Coffins. Complete with gummy worms spilling out from the sides; they'll be sure to please even teens too cool to dress up.

What better way to enjoy the fireworks than with Chocolate Chip Stars? And Christmas provides several opportunities for festive sandwiches – Flocked Trees, sandwiches decorated to look like drums or the sophisticated Fruitcake Delights will please your December guests.

MINT CHIP VALENTINES

What better way to show your love on Valentine's Day or any other time of year? Refreshing mint ice cream paired with a chewy brownie base makes a winning combination. Store-bought mint choc-chip ice cream works well but if you can't find it or prefer your own home-made ice cream, you can swirl a couple of spoonfuls of crème de menthe liqueur and 30g (⅓ cup) chocolate flakes into vanilla ice cream.

Makes 4 large or 6 medium sandwiches

1 batch of Chewy Chocolate Brownie dough (see p. 82)
500ml (1 pint) store-bought mint choc-chip ice cream
100g (4oz) plain (semi-sweet) chocolate
4 tbsp (¼ cup) mini chocolate chips, flakes or chocolate sprinkles,
　　to decorate (optional)

1. Follow the recipe on p. 82 for making the brownie base. As soon as you take the brownie tin out of the oven, use a heart-shaped cookie cutter to cut shapes. But do not remove from the tin. Use all available surface but take care not to overlap.
2. Once you've finished cutting, set the tin on a rack to cool. Take the ice cream out of the freezer to soften. Set a timer for 10 minutes to check its progress.
3. Make the topping by melting the plain chocolate in a small heatproof bowl in the microwave, on 80 per cent power for 45 seconds, then stirring well. Repeat for further periods of 20 seconds at a time until fully melted, stirring at each interval. Alternatively, put the heatproof bowl over a pan of hot (not boiling) water and stir until completely melted. Set aside to cool while you assemble the hearts.
4. Once the brownie shapes are cool, use a flat spatula to lift them carefully onto your work surface. Scoop the desired amount of ice cream onto the middle of one brownie, on the side that was touching the tin. With an angled spatula, gently spread the ice cream evenly outward towards the edges. (Use your clean cookie cutter over the brownie as a guide.) Wipe the back of the spatula before evening out the 'walls' of the ice cream. Gently place another brownie heart, tin-side down, on top.
5. Working quickly, dip half the assembled sandwich (bow to tip) into the melted chocolate. Avoid letting it sit too long or the ice cream will melt. If a thicker coat is desired, let the first coat harden before you re-dip. If desired, before the chocolate dip hardens, sprinkle on the mini chips, flakes or chocolate sprinkles.
6. Place each sandwich, without stacking, in an airtight plastic container and freeze for at least 20 minutes or until firm before serving.

MERRY DRUMS

When you've got guests during the Christmas season, these sandwiches will help to set the scene and make for a festive occasion. You can substitute your favourite ice cream to fill them – with the added sweetness from the icing you may find a more tangy flavour such as mascarpone, lemon or orange provides the best balance. If you don't have a circular cookie cutter, use the rim of a glass as a guide, cutting around it with the tip of a dull knife.

Makes 6 sandwiches

1 batch (there will be spare) of Rolled Vanilla Cookie dough (see p. 80)
Butter, for greasing
Flour, for rolling
1 batch of Mascarpone Ice Cream (see p. 114) or flavour of your choice
30g (¼ cup) icing sugar, for rolling
450g (1lb) sugarpaste

For the drum decorations
1–2 fruit winders (fruit roll), red or green
12 pretzel sticks
12 small American hard gums (gum drops)

1. Make the cookie dough as directed on p. 80 and divide into two halves, flattening each into a disc. Wrap in cling film and chill for at least 30 minutes.
2. Preheat the oven to 180°C (350°F), Gas Mark 4. Grease a cookie sheet. With a rolling pin, roll out one disc of chilled dough at a time on a floured surface until the dough is about 5mm (¼ in) thick. Roll into a circular shape.
3. Using a circle cookie cutter, cut out an even number of cookies. Repeat with the remaining dough, re-rolling as needed. You can use any extra dough to make extra cookies or freeze it for another time.
4. Space the cookies at least 1cm (½ in) apart on the cookie sheet and bake for 6–9 minutes until the edges are just starting to brown. Remove from the sheet and leave to cool.
5. Allow the ice cream to soften while preparing the icing. On a surface sprinkled with icing sugar, roll out the sugarpaste until a thickness of about 5mm (¼ in). Cut out strips of sugarpaste using a straight edge to ensure an even width. The width should match the thickness of your finished ice cream sandwiches; this will depend on the desired thickness of the ice cream layer, but should be about 3.5cm (1¼ in).

6. Use the same cutter or guide as used for the cookies to cut 12 sugarpaste circles. Set aside.
7. Apply a layer of softened ice cream about 2cm (¾in) thick to one cookie, on the side that was touching the cookie sheet. Smooth the edges with an angled spatula or dull knife and add a second cookie, sheet-side down.
8. Quickly apply the sugarpaste circles to the top and bottom of the ice cream sandwich, moistening slightly with water if needed to help adhere, then apply a long strip around the edges to join them. (You can do this by rolling the sandwich along the strip and cutting off any extra to use for the next sandwich.)
9. Place each sandwich in an airtight plastic container and place in the freezer (without stacking) while you ice the others and prepare the drum decorations.

For the drum decorations
1. Unroll the fruit leather and cut strips that are 4–4.5cm (1¾–2in) long. Lightly moisten one side of each strip with water and apply in a zig-zag fashion around the sides of the drums.
2. Insert each pretzel stick into the (flat) bottom of a gum drop to form drumsticks. To serve, lay two drumsticks on top of each sandwich, crossing them over.

FLOCKED TREES

These make an inventive alternative to Christmas cookies for when guests come round. And if you have children, they'll be more than happy to pitch in with the decoration of the cookies, especially if they're allowed to sample ...! As the icing needs time to dry, you are best off making and decorating the cookies a day ahead. You can follow instructions as below or use a Christmas tree cookie cutter if available.

Makes 6 sandwiches

1 batch of Rolled Vanilla Cookie dough (see p. 80)
Butter, for greasing
Flour, for rolling
90g (¾ cup) icing sugar
Few drops of almond extract
Few drops of green food colouring
Hundreds and thousands, coloured sprinkles, coloured sugar or other edible
    decorations
500ml (1 pint) ice cream, flavour of your choice

1. Make the cookie dough as directed on p. 80 and divide into two halves, flattening each into a disc. Wrap in cling film and chill for at least 30 minutes.
2. Preheat the oven to 180°C (350°F), Gas Mark 4. Grease a cookie sheet. With a rolling pin, roll out one disc of chilled dough at a time on a floured surface until the dough is about 5mm (¼in) thick. Roll into a circular shape.
3. Either cut with a Christmas tree cutter – measuring about 10–13cm (4–5in) – or, if you don't have one, cut out a perfect circle about 20cm (8in) in diameter with the tip of a dull knife. You can use the rim of a mixing bowl as a guide. Remove the bowl and cut all the way across the diameter of the circle, through the centre. Make two more cuts like this, equally spaced, so that you have six equally sized triangles (with rounded bottom edges).
4. Repeat with the remaining dough then space the shapes at least 1cm (½in) apart on the cookie sheet and bake until the edges are just starting to brown – about 8 minutes. Remove from the sheet and cool.

5. Prepare the icing by mixing the icing sugar with the almond extract and a few drops of green colouring, then add water a few drops at a time until you have a consistency that is thick but still workable.
6. Either drizzle or pipe the icing onto the top side of half the triangles in a zig-zag pattern, starting at the tree top. Immediately sprinkle with your chosen decoration (it will only stick to the icing within a minute of applying it to the cookie). If you sprinkle either over a bowl or on parchment paper, you can capture the fallen sprinkles and re-use them on another cookie.
7. Allow the icing to dry for at least 1 hour before assembling the ice cream sandwiches, although overnight is better.
8. Allow the ice cream to soften, then apply a layer about 2cm (¾in) thick to a non-iced cookie, on the side that was touching the cookie sheet. Smooth the edges with an angled spatula or dull knife and carefully (holding its edges) add an iced and decorated cookie, with the non-decorated side facing down.
9. Serve immediately or freeze in airtight plastic containers (without stacking).

CHOCOLATE CHIP STARS

When it's time for fireworks, serve up quintessential chocolate-chip ice cream sandwiches cut into star shapes. For more spark, you can add coloured sprinkles to the edges. If you don't have mini chips to hand, simply chop regular-sized chips, but be sure to measure by volume after chopping. These can also be made with an ice cream sandwich mould instead of a cookie cutter.

Makes 6 medium sandwiches

640ml (2⅔ cups) whipping or double cream, divided
100g (½ cup) granulated white sugar
Pinch of salt
⅓ vanilla pod (optional)
1 tsp pure vanilla extract
85g (½ cup) mini chocolate chips
12 All-American Chocolate Chip Cookies (see p. 88)
Coloured sprinkles, to decorate (optional)

1. In a small saucepan over a low heat, scald, but do not boil, 160ml (⅔ cup) of the cream. Remove from the heat and vigorously stir in the sugar and salt until dissolved. If using the vanilla pod, add now and leave to soak. Allow the mixture to come to room temperature, then remove the vanilla pod, scrape the seeds into the mixture and discard the pod. Chill in the refrigerator.
2. Once cold, add the remaining cream and the vanilla extract and stir. Put in an ice-cream maker, and follow the manufacturer's instructions. When nearly ready for the final few rotations, drop in the mini chocolate chips. Once ready, decant into an airtight plastic container and freeze for at least 1½ hours.
3. Meanwhile, follow the recipe for the All-American Chocolate Chip Cookies (see p. 88). After baking and while still quite warm, use a star-shaped cookie cutter to cut out an even number of star shapes, fitting one right next to the other but avoiding the very edges of the tin, which tend to be crunchier. After cutting all of them, carefully remove from the tin once still slightly warm and allow to cool on a rack.
4. Once completely cool, replace the cutter over one cookie. Cover with ice cream, using a small angled spatula to ensure it spreads across the entire shape. Remove the cutter and cover the ice cream with a second cookie, tin-side down. Press very gently just until it adheres. Repeat with the rest of the cookies.
5. Shake coloured sprinkles onto the edges if desired and serve immediately or place in airtight plastic containers. If you must stack use greaseproof between layers.

FRUITCAKE DELIGHTS

Christmas fruitcake has been enjoyed by generations during the festive season. This recipe, packed with toasted hazelnuts, pecans and walnuts as well as candied fruits, incorporates the best bits but leaves aside the less universally popular ingredients like rum and sultanas. Combined with Marmalade Ice Cream, these bite-sized gems make a festive treat that's easy to enjoy even while mingling at a gathering.

Makes 24 mini sandwiches

48 Fruitcake Cookies (see p. 102)
1 batch of Marmalade Ice Cream (see p. 115)

1. Make the Fruitcake Cookies as per the recipe on p. 102. Once completely cool, remove and discard the paper case from each cookie.
2. Make the Marmalade Ice Cream as per p. 115 but do not freeze it.
3. Place a small dollop of filling on the flat side of a Fruitcake Cookie and gently place a second cookie on top, flat-side down. Store – without stacking – in an airtight plastic container and freeze for at least 1½ hours before serving.

CELEBRATION CAKE SANDWICHES

What could be better for a birthday or other special celebration than ice cream, cake and buttercream all rolled into one!? You can substitute six slices of Banana Bread (see p. 106) or even your favourite loaf cake for a children's party treat.

Makes 6 sandwiches

6 slices of Mocha Loaf (see p. 108)
60g (¼ cup) butter, at room temperature
230–260g (2– 2¼ cups) icing sugar
2 tbsp milk, at room temperature
½ tsp pure vanilla extract
Few drops of food colouring (optional)
500ml (1 pint) ice cream, flavour of your choice
25g (2 tbsp) coloured or chocolate sprinkles, to decorate (optional)

1. Make the Mocha Loaf as described on p. 108 and allow to cool fully before slicing.
2. Meanwhile, prepare the buttercream. In a small bowl, use an electric mixer to beat the butter with the icing sugar at a low speed until incorporated. Scrape down the sides of the bowl and add the milk and vanilla extract, beating at a medium–high speed until light and fluffy. Set aside.
3. If you wish the tops of the sandwiches to be decorated, set aside a portion of buttercream and add a few drops of your desired food colouring, mixing with a fork to incorporate. Load into a piping bag with an icing nozzle if you wish to pipe a design or message.
4. Allow the ice cream to soften at room temperature. With an angled spatula, apply a thin layer of buttercream to one side of each slice of the Mocha Loaf then cut each slice evenly down the centre. Apply a generous layer of ice cream on top of the buttercream on one half-piece of each slice. Place the matching half, buttercream-side down, on top of the ice cream.
5. If desired, spread the colourful buttercream on top or pipe a message or pattern. (The sandwiches will be easier to eat if you keep the icing on top just in the centre.) Add sprinkles if desired – they will help prevent the icing from smearing or running.
6. Serve immediately or quickly place in an airtight plastic container, without stacking, and freeze.

GRAVEYARD COFFINS

Sure to delight children and adults at your next Halloween party, these scary coffins are easier to make than you might think! You can make your own writing icing by combining 30g (¼ cup) icing sugar with a few drops of water, and stirring until very smooth. Use to fill a piping bag with a writing nozzle, or at a pinch use a strong, zip-lock, plastic food storage bag with a very small hole snipped off one corner.

Makes 5 sandwiches

1 batch of Chocolate Ice Cream (see p. 112) or 500ml (1 pint) premium
   store-bought, softened
10 Chewy Chocolate Brownies (see p. 82)
20 gummy worms or gummy body parts
1 tube of white writing icing

1. Make and bake the brownies as per the recipe on p. 82. Cut the brownie base while still warm from the oven, making 10 rectangles. Avoid using the very edges that are touching the sides of the tin.
2. Match up rectangles, placing them tin-side to tin-side. Cut off the corners, following the basic shape shown in the photo here.
3. Spread the desired amount of softened ice cream onto the tin-side of one coffin brownie. Smooth the edges with an angled spatula or a smooth knife. Place four gummy sweets across the ice cream so that they are sticking out over the edge of the coffin.
4. Smooth a very thin layer of ice cream on the tin-side of the matching coffin brownie and quickly put it over the ice cream and the gummy sweets. Quickly place in an airtight plastic container – without stacking – and freeze until ready to serve. Just before serving, use the writing icing to pipe your desired 'epitaph' onto the coffin, such as 'R.I.P.' or 'Here lies ...' and your guest's name!

THE COOKIE RECIPES

Here are cookie ideas to complement almost any season or occasion. Why not try a light and crunchy Vanilla Meringue or a moist and tender Grated Apple Cookie? Both of these combine well with creamy or fruity fillings. And for coconut-lovers, nothing beats a chunky Coconut Macaroon, which, paired with a chocolate ice cream, will satiate the most ardent craving.

This section also presents a few alternatives to conventional cookies: trendy Madeleines, much-loved Banana Bread and a sophisticated Mocha Loaf. Although these alternatives can be frozen, you may find it best to make, slice and fill them right before serving,

Whichever your predilection, you will find something here to go perfectly with your favourite ice cream or sorbet.

ROLLED VANILLA COOKIES

Makes 16–24 cookies

225g (1 cup) butter
110g (½ cup) soft light brown sugar, firmly packed
100g (½ cup) granulated white sugar
1 egg
1½ tsp pure vanilla extract
5½ tsp milk
350g (2½ cups) plain (all-purpose) flour, plus extra for rolling
5g (1 tsp) baking powder
Coloured sugar or sprinkles, to decorate (optional)

> **NOTE:** If you wish to substitute almond extract for vanilla, decrease to
> 1 teaspoon and increase the milk to 2 tablespoons.

1. In a large bowl, use an electric mixer with the beaters or paddle to cream the butter. Add both types of sugar and the egg, and mix until creamy.
2. Beat in the vanilla extract and milk and continue beating until well mixed. Add the flour and baking powder and beat on a low speed until well incorporated.
3. Divide the dough into two parts; flatten each to about 1cm (½in) thick. Cover in cling film (plastic wrap) and refrigerate until firm (about 2 hours).
4. Preheat the oven to 200°C (400°F), Gas Mark 6. Roll out the dough on a lightly floured surface, one disc at a time, to 1cm (½in) thickness. Cut with the desired shape of cutter. Wiggle the cutter slightly to ensure a clean outline.
5. Place the cookies 2.5cm (1in) apart onto ungreased cookie sheets. At this stage, coloured sugar or sprinkles may be added to the unbaked cookies; press it on lightly. Bake for 6–9 minutes, until the edges are just lightly brown. Immediately remove from the cookie sheet onto a cooling rack and allow to cool completely before filling or storing in an airtight container.

CHEWY CHOCOLATE BROWNIES

Makes 8–12 brownies

110g (½ cup) butter or margarine, plus extra for greasing
60g (2 x 1oz squares) unsweetened baking chocolate, 90% cocoa solids (or see tip)
200g (1 cup) granulated white sugar
2 eggs
1½ tsp pure vanilla extract
70g (½ cup) plain (all-purpose) flour
Pinch of salt

1. Preheat the oven to 180°C (350°F), Gas Mark 4. Lightly grease a 38 x 25 x 2cm (15 x 10 x 1in) baking tin.
2. Put the butter or margarine and the chocolate in a medium heatproof bowl. Microwave on medium heat (70 per cent power) for 1 minute. Stir together and repeat until completely melted. Alternatively, you can melt the two ingredients in a heatproof bowl set over a pan of simmering water (a double boiler), stirring until melted.
3. Add the sugar to the chocolate mixture and stir. Allow to cool slightly, then add the eggs and vanilla, stirring with a fork until completely incorporated. Add the flour and salt and stir until just incorporated.
4. Spread the batter evenly across the tin, using an angled spatula or the back of a spoon to ensure it is evenly distributed. Any other ingredients which are to be baked in for variations (e.g. digestive biscuits if making S'mores) should be added now.
5. Bake for 10–12 minutes. The centre should be firm but still slightly moist and the edges *may* start to pull away from the sides of the tin. Do not overcook. Remove from the oven and cut with a knife or use shaped cutters immediately while still hot. Allow to cool before filling or storing in an airtight container.

TIP: Using chocolate with 90 per cent cocoa solids makes these brownies really dark and chocolatey. If you can't get hold of it and your chocolate has a smaller percentage of cocoa solids, we recommend you add 2 tablespoons of cocoa powder and reduce the sugar by 2 tablespoons.

BUTTERSCOTCH BROWNIES

Makes 8–12 brownies

60g (¼ cup) butter, plus extra for greasing
220g (1 cup) soft light brown sugar, firmly packed
1 egg
1½ tsp pure vanilla extract
110g (¾ cup) plain (all-purpose) flour
¾ tsp baking powder
¼ tsp bicarbonate of soda
¼ tsp salt
150g (¾ cup) finely chopped dates (about 12–14 pieces), sprinkled with 1 tbsp flour
if moist to prevent sticking (also see tip below)

1. Preheat the oven to 180°C (350°F), Gas Mark 4. Grease a 23cm (9in) square baking tin.
2. In a small heatproof bowl, melt the butter in the microwave, using 80 per cent power for 20–30 seconds. Alternatively, put the heatproof bowl over a pan of hot (not boiling) water and stir until completely melted. Stir in the brown sugar until dissolved. Allow to cool slightly then beat in the egg and vanilla extract with a hand whisk until well incorporated.
3. In a separate bowl, whisk the flour, baking powder, bicarbonate of soda and salt. Gradually stir into the sugar mixture. Also add the dates. Spread into the greased tin, using an angled spatula or the back of a spoon to ensure it is evenly distributed, and bake for 18–20 minutes. Cut into your desired shapes while still warm. Allow to cool before filling or storing in an airtight container.

TIP: If your dates are not very moist, cut into bits and put into a small pan along with 2 tablespoons of water and cook over a low heat, stirring constantly, until they form a soft paste. Cool before adding to the mixture as normal, but without the added 1 tablespoon of flour.

SNICKERDOODLE COOKIES

Makes 12 cookies

For the dough
210g (1½ cups) plain (all-purpose) flour
1 tsp baking powder
¼ tsp salt
110g (½ cup) butter, at room temperature
100g (½ cup) granulated white sugar
55g (¼ cup) soft light brown sugar, firmly packed
1 large egg
¾ tsp pure vanilla extract

For the cookie coating
65g (⅓ cup) granulated white sugar
2 tsp ground cinnamon
Flour or icing sugar, if needed

1. In a large bowl, whisk together the flour, baking powder and salt. Using an electric mixer with the beaters or paddle, beat the butter and sugars until smooth (about 3 minutes). Stop the mixer and scrape down the sides of the bowl once or twice as necessary.
2. Add the egg, beating well, then beat in the vanilla extract. Add the dry mixture in two parts, beating until smooth. Cover and refrigerate until firm enough to roll into balls (45–60 minutes).
3. Preheat the oven to 200°C (400°F), Gas Mark 6. Place a rack in the centre of the oven and line two baking sheets with parchment paper. For the cookie coating, mix together the sugar and cinnamon in a small bowl.
4. Shape the dough into 3.5cm (1¼in) balls, then roll the balls in the coating mixture one at a time and place on the prepared sheets about 7.5cm (3in) apart. Using the bottom of a glass, gently flatten each cookie evenly to about 1cm (½in) thick. If the cookies begin to stick to the glass, lightly coat the glass in flour or icing sugar between each cookie.
5. Bake the cookies for 8–10 minutes or until the edges are light golden brown. Remove from the oven, wait for 1 minute and, using a spatula, place on a wire rack to cool. These cookies can be stored in an airtight container at room temperature for about 1 week.

VANILLA MERINGUES

Makes 16 meringues

3 large egg whites (½ cup)
Pinch of salt
¼ tsp cream of tartar
200g (1 cup) granulated white sugar
½ tsp vinegar or fresh lemon juice
1½ tsp pure vanilla extract
Assortment of sprinkles, to decorate (optional)

For chocolate meringues (optional)
1 tbsp cocoa powder
110g (½ cup) chocolate chips

1. Using an electric mixer with the whisk attachment, beat the egg whites and salt in a large bowl until frothy. Add the cream of tartar and continue whisking as you lightly sprinkle the sugar over the egg whites until it is completely added. Add the vinegar (or lemon juice) and vanilla extract (and cocoa powder, if desired) and whisk until stiff peaks form and the mixture is glossy.
2. Line two baking sheets with parchment paper and turn the oven on to its lowest setting – about 90–100°C (200–210°F), Gas Mark ¼.
3. Take a clean piping bag and insert a large-mouthed nozzle in your desired shape (a smooth, round nozzle works well). If you don't have a piping bag and icing nozzle, you can use a large zip-lock plastic bag and snip a small hole (about 1cm or ½in) across one bottom corner.
4. Pipe meringues onto the lined baking sheets in spirals, starting in the centre and working outward until each one is the desired size, using all the meringue mixture. Be sure to allow a bit of space between the meringues as they expand slightly in the oven. Apply sprinkle decorations or chocolate chips – ensure the chips adhere to the meringues by gently pressing them in as needed.
5. Bake for 2–2½ hours. After this time, do not remove from the oven, but turn the oven off, leaving the door closed and the meringues inside until cold. You can leave them in the oven overnight if you wish. Use as required or store the meringues in an airtight container.

ALL-AMERICAN CHOCOLATE CHIP COOKIES

Makes 8–12 cookies

225g (1 cup) butter, plus extra for greasing
220g (1 cup) soft light brown sugar, firmly packed
100g (½ cup) granulated white sugar
2 eggs
1½ tsp pure vanilla extract
315g (2¼ cups) plain (all-purpose) flour
1 tsp salt
1 tsp bicarbonate of soda
340g (2 cups) plain (semi-sweet) chocolate chips

1. Preheat the oven to 180°C (350°F), Gas Mark 4. Lightly grease a 38 x 25 x 2cm (15 x 10 x 1in) baking tin.
2. In a medium bowl, use an electric mixer with the beaters or paddle to cream the butter. Add both types of sugar and mix until light and fluffy. Beat in the eggs and vanilla extract. Sift in the flour, salt and bicarbonate of soda and stir to incorporate.
3. Stir in the chocolate chips then spread the batter evenly across the greased tin, using an angled spatula or the back of a spoon to ensure it is evenly distributed.
4. Bake for 12–15 minutes. The edges should look golden and the centre appear firm. Do not overcook. Remove from the oven and, while still warm, use shaped cutters immediately to cut through the cookie dough. Jiggle the cutter slightly to achieve a clean line. Remove the cut-outs when cooled. Use as required or store in an airtight container.

SOFT OATMEAL COOKIES

Makes 16 cookies

115g (½ cup) butter
160g (¾ cup) soft light brown sugar, firmly packed
50g (¼ cup) granulated white sugar
1 egg
1 tsp pure vanilla extract
1 tbsp milk
140g (1 cup) plain (all-purpose) flour
½ tsp baking powder
½ tsp bicarbonate of soda
½ tsp salt
75g (1 cup) oatmeal
1 tsp cinnamon
½ tsp ground nutmeg, allspice or pumpkin pie spices (optional)
8 tbsp (½ cup) raisins, nuts, chocolate chips, coconut or combination (optional)

1. Preheat the oven to 180°C (350°F), Gas Mark 4.
2. In a large bowl, use an electric mixer with the beaters or paddle to cream the butter. Add both types of sugar and mix until creamy. Beat in the egg, vanilla extract and milk and continue beating until well mixed.
3. Add the flour, baking powder, bicarbonate of soda and salt. Beat on a low speed until well incorporated.
4. Add the oatmeal, cinnamon and any desired spices and/or other optional ingredients and mix on a low speed just until incorporated.
5. Using a small ice-cream scoop if possible (or measure out 2 tablespoons per cookie), drop heaps of the mixture 4cm (1½in) apart onto ungreased cookie sheets. Aim to use the same amount for each cookie so that the halves will match up.
6. Bake for 9–11 minutes, until the edges are just lightly brown. Immediately remove from the cookie sheet on to a cooling rack and allow to cool completely before filling or storing in an airtight container.

GRATED APPLE COOKIES

Makes 12 large cookies

55g (¼ cup) butter, plus extra for greasing
150g (⅔ cup) soft light brown sugar, firmly packed
1 egg
1 tsp pure vanilla extract
140g (1 cup) plain (all-purpose) flour
½ tsp baking powder
¼ tsp bicarbonate of soda
¼ tsp salt
¾ tsp cinnamon
¼ tsp nutmeg
2 tbsp apple juice
50g (½ cup) chopped lightly toasted walnuts
60g (½ cup) raisins (optional)
125g (½ cup) grated tart apple, such as Granny Smith (about 1½ apples)

1. Preheat the oven to 200°C (400°F), Gas Mark 6. Grease a couple of cookie sheets.
2. In a large bowl, use an electric mixer with the beaters or paddle to cream the butter and sugar together until well combined. Beat in the egg and vanilla extract until well mixed.
3. In a separate bowl, whisk together the flour, baking powder, bicarbonate of soda, salt, cinnamon and nutmeg. Add to the creamed mixture in three parts, alternating with additions of the apple juice. Stir in the nuts, raisins and apple.
4. Drop by teaspoons onto the greased cookie sheets, leaving 4–5cm (1½–2in) between each cookie. Bake for 9–11 minutes. Immediately remove from the cookie sheet onto a cooling rack and allow to cool completely before filling or storing in an airtight container.

SOFT GINGER COOKIES

Makes 16 cookies

90g (¼ cup + 2 tbsp) butter
200g (1 cup) granulated white sugar
1 egg
45ml (¼ cup) golden syrup (light molasses)
280g (2 cups) plain (all-purpose) flour
2 tsp bicarbonate of soda
½ tsp salt
1½ tsp ground ginger
1¼ tsp ground cinnamon

1. In a large bowl, use an electric mixer with the beaters or paddle to cream the butter and 150g (⅔ cup) of the sugar until well combined. Beat in the egg and syrup (molasses) until well combined.
2. In a separate bowl, stir together the dry ingredients and add to the creamed mixture, blending until combined. Refrigerate the dough for 2 hours.
3. Preheat the oven to 180°C (350°F), Gas Mark 4. Roll the dough into balls about 4cm (1½in) in diameter. Roll each ball in the remaining granulated sugar. Use the bottom of a glass to flatten each cookie to about 8cm (3in) in diameter.
4. Bake on ungreased cookie sheets, 5cm (2in) apart, for 7–8 minutes or until the cookies are puffed and the tops are cracked. Remove immediately onto a cooling rack, allowing space between each cookie; they will flatten as they cool. Once cool, use as required or store in an airtight container.

WHITE CHOCOLATE CHIP COOKIES

Makes 8–12 cookies

180g (¾ cup) butter, plus extra for greasing
220g (1 cup) soft light brown sugar, firmly packed
100g (½ cup) granulated white sugar
2 eggs
1 tsp pure vanilla extract
315g (2¼ cups) plain (all-purpose) flour
1 tsp salt
1 tsp bicarbonate of soda
340g (2 cups) white chocolate chips

1. Preheat the oven to 180°C (350°F), Gas Mark 4.
2. In a medium bowl, use an electric mixer with the beaters or paddle to cream the butter. Add both types of sugar and mix until light and fluffy. Beat in the eggs and vanilla extract. Sift in the flour, salt and bicarbonate of soda and mix to incorporate. Stir in the white chocolate chips.
3. If you want to make cut-out shapes, lightly grease a 38 x 25 x 2cm (15 x 10 x 1in) baking tin. Spread the dough evenly across the tin with an angled spatula. Bake for 10–12 minutes or until the centre is cooked and the edges only lightly brown. Remove from the oven and cut into shapes with your desired cutter while still hot.
4. For round cookies, lightly grease a flat cookie sheet. Drop even amounts of the dough from an ice-cream scoop (about 2 tablespoons) with at least 4cm (1½in) between each. Bake for 8–10 minutes until the centre is cooked and the edges only slightly brown. Be careful not to overcook. Allow to cool completely before filling or storing in an airtight container.

PUMPKIN SPICE COOKIES

Makes 12–16 cookies

40g (½ cup) oats
140g (1 cup) plain (all-purpose) flour
½ tsp bicarbonate of soda
¼ tsp salt
1 tsp ground cinnamon
¼ tsp ground nutmeg
110g (½ cup) butter, plus extra for greasing
110g (½ cup) soft light brown sugar, firmly packed
75g (¼ cup + 2 tbsp) granulated white sugar
1 egg, slightly beaten
½ tsp pure vanilla extract
120g (½ cup) canned pumpkin purée
80g (½ cup) plain (semi-sweet) chocolate chips

> **NOTE:** Canned pumpkin purée is concentrated; if substituting home-made pumpkin purée, ensure you have drained off as much moisture as possible by sieving and packing down.

1. Preheat the oven to 180°C (350°F), Gas Mark 4. Grease a couple of cookie sheets.
2. In a medium bowl, combine the oats, flour, bicarbonate of soda, salt and both ground spices. In another large bowl, use an electric mixer to cream the butter, then gradually add both types of sugar. Beat until light and fluffy – this takes 2–3 minutes. Add the egg and vanilla extract and incorporate well.
3. Add alternate additions of the dry ingredients and the pumpkin purée, mixing well after each. Then stir in the chocolate chips.
4. Using a small ice-cream scoop, (or measure out 2 tablespoons per cookie), drop heaps of the mixture onto the greased cookie sheets. Bake for 12–15 minutes, until firm and just lightly brown. Immediately remove from the cookie sheet onto a cooling rack and allow to cool completely before filling or storing in an airtight container.

COCONUT MACAROONS

Makes 16 medium cookies

2 egg whites
300g (3 cups) desiccated coconut
1½ tsp almond extract
Pinch of salt
200g (⅔ cup) sweetened condensed milk
Few drops of red food colouring (optional)
Icing sugar, if needed

1. Preheat the oven to 180°C (350°F), Gas Mark 4. Line a couple of cookie sheets with parchment paper.
2. In a small bowl, whip the egg whites with an electric mixer, until stiff. Set aside.
3. Put the coconut, almond extract, salt, sweetened condensed milk and food colouring, if desired, in a medium bowl and stir until combined. Fold in the whipped egg whites until combined. Using a medium-sized mashed-potato scoop, take scoopfuls of the mixture, packing in tightly by pressing against the side of the bowl or with another spoon. Drop flat-side down onto the parchment-lined sheets.
4. Use the palm of your hand or the bottom of a glass dipped in icing sugar to gently flatten each scoop into a round, about 1cm (½in) high. The macaroons will spread very little in the oven.
5. Bake for 8 minutes and remove from the oven. Leave on the cookie sheet for at least 5 minutes. Fill only once completely cooled, or store in an airtight container.

    TIP: For a milder flavour, try substituting vanilla extract for the almond. The macaroons will come out a golden cream shade.

BEVERLY HILLS COOKIES

Makes 18 cookies

120g (½ cup) butter
110g (½ cup) soft light brown sugar, firmly packed
100g (½ cup) granulated white sugar
1 egg
½ tsp pure vanilla extract
140g (1 cup) plain (all-purpose) flour, plus extra for flattening the cookies
110g (1½ cups) oatmeal, whizzed to a fine powder (1¼ cups after blending) in blender
    or food processor (If using store-bought, take it out of the freezer to soften for 3–4
    minutes only, or microwave on 80 per cent power for 10–15 seconds.)
½ tsp baking powder
½ tsp bicarbonate of soda
¼ tsp salt
170g (1 cup) plain (semi-sweet) chocolate chips
85g (3oz) plain (semi-sweet) chocolate, grated
75g (¾ cup) walnuts, toasted then chopped (optional)

1. Preheat the oven to 190°C (375°F), Gas Mark 5.
2. With an electric mixer, beat together the butter and both types of sugar until
   creamy. Beat in the egg and vanilla extract until light and fluffy.
3. In a separate bowl, whisk the flour, fine oatmeal, baking powder, bicarbonate of soda
   and salt. Gradually add to the creamed mixture. Stir in the chocolate chips, grated
   chocolate and walnuts, if using.
4. Roll the dough into 4cm (1½in) balls. Place them 5cm (2in) apart on an ungreased
   cookie sheet. Use the bottom of a glass to flatten to about 7–8cm (approx. 3in).
   To prevent sticking, dip the glass in flour between each one.
5. Bake for 8–9 minutes. Remove immediately and cool completely on a wire rack.
   Use as required or store in an airtight container.

AMARETTO BISCUITS

Makes 16 biscuits

250g (1 cup) marzipan (almond paste)
200g (1 cup) caster sugar (superfine granulated)
2–3 egg whites
¼ tsp almond extract
2–3 drops of red food colouring (optional)

1. Preheat the oven to 170°C (325°F), Gas Mark 3. Line a cookie sheet with parchment paper.
2. Cut up the marzipan into small bits and put into a medium bowl. Gradually knead in the sugar. Gradually knead in the egg whites (you may need more or less, depending on the consistency), almond extract and colouring, if desired, until the mixture is uniform and smooth.
3. Spoon out or use a piping bag to pipe even amounts – about 1 teaspoonful – onto the lined cookie sheet, allowing a full 5cm (2in) between each. These really spread!
4. Bake for 20–25 minutes. Remove and allow to cool before removing from the paper. If the paper sticks, lightly moisten the back of it with a damp tea towel, wait a minute and then peel away. Use as required or store in an airtight container.

TIN ROOF COOKIES

Makes 12 cookies

60g (¼ cup) butter, plus extra for greasing
110g (½ cup) soft light brown sugar, firmly packed
50g (¼ cup) granulated white sugar
1 egg
170g (½ cup) peanut butter, preferably chunky
¼ tsp bicarbonate of soda
¼ tsp salt
½ tsp pure vanilla extract
140–175g (1–1¼ cups) plain (all-purpose) flour
85g (¼ cup + 2 tbsp) plain (semi-sweet) chocolate chips

1. Preheat the oven to 190°C (375°F), Gas Mark 5. Grease a couple of cookie sheets.
2. With an electric mixer, beat the butter and both types of sugar until creamy. Beat in the egg, peanut butter, bicarbonate of soda, salt and vanilla extract until well combined.
3. Add the flour to the creamed mixture and blend well. Use the greater amount of flour if your peanut butter is especially oily. Stir in the chocolate chips.
4. Using a small ice-cream or mashed-potato scoop (or measure out 2 tablespoons of mixture), drop heaps of dough 7–8cm (approx. 3in) apart onto the greased cookie sheets. Use the bottom of a glass to flatten the cookies.
5. Bake for 10–12 minutes. Remove immediately and cool completely on a wire rack. Use as required or store in an airtight container.

FRUITCAKE COOKIES

Makes 48 mini cookies

60g (¼ cup) butter
50g (¼ cup) soft light brown sugar, firmly packed
¼ tsp bicarbonate of soda
½ tsp ground cinnamon
⅛ tsp salt (about 3 pinches)
1 egg
½ tsp pure vanilla extract
90g (½ cup + 2 tbsp) plain (all-purpose) flour
125g (1 cup) pitted dates, chopped
125g (½ cup) quartered glacé cherries
100g (½ cup) diced candied pineapple
30g (¼ cup) walnuts, toasted and chopped
30g (¼ cup) pecans, toasted and chopped
35g (¼ cup) hazelnuts, toasted and chopped

1. Preheat the oven to 180°C (350°F), Gas Mark 4. Either fill mini cupcake trays with 30 paper cake cases or alternatively use 30 lined foil petit-four cups on a cookie sheet.
2. In a medium bowl, use an electric mixer to beat the butter, sugar, bicarbonate of soda, cinnamon and salt until blended. Add the egg and vanilla extract and beat until fluffy.
3. In a separate bowl, mix the flour with the dates, glacé cherries and pineapple until coated. Stir this mixture and the nuts into the butter mixture until blended.
4. Drop small spoonfuls into the liners or baking cups until half-full only. Bake for 11–13 minutes until the tops look dry and the edges are beginning to brown. Leave on a cooling rack until completely cool.

MOCHA COOKIES

Makes 12 cookies

120g (½ cup) butter, plus extra for greasing
100g (½ cup) granulated white sugar
55g (¼ cup) soft light brown sugar, firmly packed
1 tsp pure vanilla extract
1 tbsp instant espresso powder
1 egg
120g (⅞ cup) plain (all-purpose) flour
40g (¼ cup + 2 tbsp) unsweetened cocoa powder
¼ tsp salt
100g (½ cup) milk chocolate chips
50g (¼ cup) chopped pecans, toasted

1. Preheat the oven to 180°C (350°F), Gas Mark 4 and grease a cookie sheet.
2. Using an electric mixer with the beaters or paddle, beat the butter, both types of sugar, vanilla extract and espresso powder until incorporated. Scrape down the sides of the bowl with a rubber spatula then beat on high speed until fluffy, for about 3 minutes.
3. Add the egg and beat well, scraping down the sides of the bowl as needed. Add the flour, cocoa and salt and beat until blended, then add the chocolate chips and nuts. Mix until incorporated.
4. Drop heaps of the mixture onto the greased cookie sheet using a small ice-cream or mashed-potato scoop (or measure out 2 tablespoons of mixture), into 12 mounds about 3cm (1¼ in) apart. Bake for 10 minutes or until the cookies appear set. Their centres should remain chewy and soft so do not overcook.
5. Once removed from the oven, allow the cookies to remain on the sheet for 1 minute before removing onto a wire rack to cool completely. Once cool, use as required or store in an airtight container.

ZESTY MADELEINES

Makes 16 small cakes

75g (⅓ cup) butter, plus extra for greasing
100g (½ cup) granulated white sugar
3 eggs
100g (¾ cup) plain (all-purpose) flour
½ tsp baking powder
1 tsp orange zest, finely grated

1. Preheat the oven to 200°C (400°F), Gas Mark 6. Lightly grease two madeleine moulds.
2. In a medium bowl, cream the butter. Add the sugar and mix well. Add the eggs one at a time, beating well after each.
3. In a separate small bowl, whisk the flour and baking powder. Stir in the orange zest until well coated.
4. Add the flour mixture to the butter mixture and incorporate well. Spoon the mixture into the moulds, place the moulds on flat cookie sheets and bake for 10–12 minutes.
5. Remove from the oven and immediately remove the madeleines from the moulds onto a cooling rack. Cool completely before cutting and filling or storing in an airtight container.

BANANA BREAD

A version of this recipe was first introduced to me by a flatmate at university, where it saw me through a number of late study nights. I've since introduced it to friends and colleagues in Mexico, France and here in the UK. My family especially loves the bread for breakfast as a delicious alternative to their usual cereals. When made into ice cream sandwiches, they are best enjoyed on the spot so that the bread remains firm.

Makes 8 servings

3 large or 4 medium, very ripe bananas
120g (½ cup) butter, plus extra for greasing
200g (1 cup) granulated white sugar
2 eggs
280g (2 cups) plain (all-purpose) flour, plus extra for the tin(s)
2 tsp bicarbonate of soda
30g (¼ cup) walnuts, chopped

1. Preheat the oven to 180°C (350°F), Gas Mark 4. Grease and flour a 22 x 11 x 7cm (8½ x 4½ x 2½in) loaf tin or six mini loaf tins.
2. In a large bowl, vigorously mix the bananas until light and fluffy, then put aside. In a medium bowl, cream the butter and sugar. Cream them some more! Then add the eggs, one at a time, beating well after each.
3. Add the flour and bicarbonate of soda and mix well. Add the mixed bananas and mix in until combined. Pour into the prepared loaf tin(s). Scatter the nuts on the top.
4. Bake on the middle shelf of the oven for 50–55 minutes if using a standard loaf tin or 25–30 minutes in mini tins. Remove from the oven and cool in the tin on a wire rack for 10 minutes before removing and allowing to cool fully. Use as required or store in an airtight container.

   TIP: If you've ever inadvertently bitten into a mouthful of bicarbonate of soda, you will know that it tends to clump. Ensure your container is fully sealed then give it a vigorous shake before opening to measure.

MOCHA LOAF

Makes 10 servings

1 tbsp instant coffee powder
60ml (¼ cup) boiling water
180g (1¼ cups) plain (all-purpose) flour, plus extra for the tin
¼ tsp salt
1½ tsp baking powder
120g (½ cup) butter, plus extra for greasing
150g (¾ cup) granulated white sugar
2 eggs
60ml (¼ cup) milk
½ tsp pure vanilla extract
100g (½ cup) plain (semi-sweet) chocolate chips

1. Preheat the oven to 180°C (350°F), Gas Mark 4. Grease and flour a 22 x 11 x 7cm (8½ x 4½ x 2½in) loaf tin.
2. Add the coffee powder to the boiling water and stir until dissolved. Leave to cool. In a medium bowl, whisk the flour, salt and baking powder and set aside.
3. With an electric mixer in a large bowl, beat the butter and sugar until creamy. Add the eggs, one at a time, beating well after each. Add in one-third of the flour mixture, mixing on a low speed until just combined. Add half the milk, half the coffee and all of the vanilla extract, mixing until combined. Repeat with the flour, milk and coffee, ending with the last third of the flour mixture.
4. Stir in the chocolate chips and pour the batter into the prepared loaf tin. Bake on the middle shelf of the oven for 50–55 minutes. Remove and cool in the tin on a wire rack for 10 minutes before removing and allowing to cool fully. Use as required or store in an airtight container.

CHOCOLATE CUPCAKES

I've included my recipe for chocolate cupcakes, which are used in my cupcake sundae and cupshake recipes. While this recipe makes a full dozen, you can always ice the extra ones or freeze for a later time.

Makes 12 cakes

85g (3oz) unsweetened chocolate, 90% cocoa solids
145g (1 cup + 2 tbsp) plain flour
¼ tsp bicarbonate of soda
¼ tsp baking powder
¼ tsp salt
120g (½ cup) butter
100g (½ cup) granulated white sugar
110g (½ cup) soft light brown sugar, firmly packed
1 egg
120ml (½ cup) buttermilk, at room temperature
1 tsp pure vanilla extract

1. Preheat the oven to 180°C (350°F), Gas Mark 4. Line a 12-hole cupcake tray with cake cases (ideally greaseproof); set aside.
2. In a heatproof bowl, melt the chocolate in the microwave at 80 per cent power for 1 minute, then stir. If needed, return to the microwave for 10 seconds at a time, stirring between each interval until smooth. Alternatively, you can put the heatproof bowl over a pan of hot (not boiling) water and stir until melted and smooth. Set aside to cool.
3. Whisk or sift the flour with the bicarbonate of soda, baking powder and salt. Set aside. In a medium bowl using an electric mixer, cream the butter and both types of sugar. Add the egg and mix until incorporated, scraping down the sides of the bowl as needed. Pour in the cooled melted chocolate and mix. In a separate jug, mix the buttermilk and vanilla extract.
4. Add alternate amounts of flour and buttermilk mixture, starting and ending with flour. Mix just until incorporated; do not over-mix or the cupcakes will be tough!
5. Divide the batter evenly among the liners, filling each about two-thirds full. Bake for 20–25 minutes, rotating the tray halfway through, until a skewer or cake tester inserted into the centre of a cake comes out clean. Allow to cool completely before adding to a cupshake or topping with ice cream.

THE ICE CREAM RECIPES

Nothing beats home-made when it comes to ice cream! When freshly prepared, the flavours really come alive. In this section I've set apart the recipes for the ice cream flavours most commonly used throughout this book. So whether you're hankering for something universal, such as vanilla or chocolate, or a lighter option like lemon or marmalade, you'll find it here. Any of the recipes can be easily prepared on its own or combined with a cookie option of your choosing.

VANILLA ICE CREAM

Makes 800ml–1 litre (1½–2 pints)

480ml (2 cups) double or whipping cream
Pinch of salt
40g (¼ cup + 2 tbsp) granulated white
   sugar
¼ vanilla pod
1 tsp vanilla extract

1. Scald one-quarter of the cream
   (120ml/½ cup) over a low heat (but
   do not boil). Add the salt and sugar
   and stir until dissolved.
2. Remove from the heat, add the vanilla
   pod and allow to soak. Then scrape
   out the seeds into the cream mixture
   and remove the pod.
3. Pour into a heatproof bowl, allow to
   come to room temperature, then chill
   in the refrigerator.
4. Once cool, add the vanilla extract
   and the rest of the cream (360ml/
   1½ cups). Pour into an ice-cream
   maker and follow the manufacturer's
   instructions. When finished churning,
   decant into an airtight plastic container and freeze for 2 hours.

CHOCOLATE ICE CREAM

Makes approx. 700ml (1½ pints)

170g (1 cup) plain (semi-sweet) chocolate
   chips
240ml (1 cup) double or whipping cream
3 egg yolks
¼ tsp salt

1. In a small heatproof bowl, melt the
   chocolate chips in the microwave on
   80% power for 1 minute. Stir and heat
   again for 10 seconds, then stir and
   repeat in 10-second increments until
   smooth. Alternatively, put the heatproof bowl over a pan of hot (not
   boiling) water and stir until melted.
2. Transfer to a medium bowl and set
   aside for 10 minutes (but no longer).
3. Meanwhile, in a separate medium bowl,
   whip the cream and set aside. Add the
   egg yolks and salt to the cooled
   chocolate and stir with a hand whisk
   until just combined.
4. Fold the cooled chocolate into the
   whipped cream mixture. Spoon into
   an airtight plastic container, allowing at
   least 1cm (½in) of empty space at the
   top of the container as the mixture
   will expand as it freezes. Allow to
   freeze for at least 1½ hours.

MOCHA ICE CREAM

Makes approx. 700ml (1½ pints)

2 tsp instant coffee granules
1 tsp boiling water
170g (½ cup) milk chocolate chips
180ml (¾ cup) double cream, divided
2 egg whites

1. In a heatproof cup, dissolve the coffee granules in the boiling water. Then combine the coffee, chocolate chips and 60ml (¼ cup) of the double cream in a small heatproof bowl.
2. Microwave on 80 per cent power for 1 minute then stir well to help the chips melt. Return to the microwave and repeat for 10-second intervals, stirring well each time until the mixture is smooth. Alternatively, you can put the heatproof bowl over a pan of hot (not boiling) water, stirring until the mixture is melted and smooth. Transfer to a larger bowl to cool for 10–15 minutes.
3. In a small, clean bowl, whisk the egg whites until stiff peaks form. Fold into the cooled chocolate mixture. In another small bowl, beat the remaining 120ml (½ cup) of the cream until stiff peaks form; also fold this into the chocolate mixture.
4. Spoon into an airtight plastic container, allowing at least 1cm (½in) of empty space at the top of the container as the mixture will expand as it freezes. Allow to freeze for at least 1½ hours.

MASCARPONE ICE CREAM

Makes 800ml–1 litre (1½–2 pints)

2 egg yolks
1 tsp cornflour (cornstarch)
80g (⅓ cup + 1 tbsp) caster sugar (superfine granulated)
75ml (¼ cup + 1 tbsp) full-fat milk
¼ tsp nutmeg
250g (1 cup) mascarpone cheese
200g (⅔ cup) fromage frais

1. In a medium bowl with an electric mixer, whisk together the yolks, cornflour and sugar until light and fluffy. Bring the milk and nutmeg to a gentle simmer in a small saucepan over a low heat.
2. Remove the warmed milk from the heat and whisk little by little into the egg mixture. Then return the entire mixture to the saucepan and bring back to a gentle simmer, whisking continuously. Do not allow to clump.
3. Remove from the heat, pour into a heatproof bowl, cover and cool to room temperature then chill in the refrigerator.
4. Once chilled, pour into an ice-cream maker, along with the mascarpone and fromage frais, and follow the manufacturer's instructions. Transfer to an airtight plastic container, allowing at least 1cm (½in) of empty space at the top of the container as the mixture will expand as it freezes. Allow to freeze for at least 2 hours.

LEMON ICE CREAM

Makes approx. 700ml (1½ pints)

360ml (1½ cups) whipping cream
115g (½ cup + 1 tbsp) granulated
  white sugar
60ml (¼ cup) fresh lemon juice
  (about 1½–2 lemons)
5 tsp grated lemon zest (about 2 lemons)

1. Put the cream, sugar, lemon juice and
   zest in a medium (but deep) bowl, and
   beat using an electric mixer with the
   beaters or paddle, until completely
   combined and slightly thickened. Be
   sure to scrape any zest off the beaters
   and stir back into the cream mixture
   with a spoon or spatula before
   freezing.
2. Pour into an airtight plastic storage
   container. Allow at least 1cm (½in) of
   empty space at the top of the container as the mixture will expand as it
   freezes. Freeze for at least 2 hours.

MARMALADE ICE CREAM

Makes approx. 460ml (1 pint)

120ml (½ cup) fine-shred orange
  marmalade
140ml (½ cup + 1 tbsp) double cream,
  chilled
120ml (½ cup) ready-to-serve custard

1. In a small microwave-proof bowl, heat
   the marmalade in the microwave, on
   80 per cent power for 30 seconds.
   Stir vigorously to break up lumps.
   Repeat for another 30 seconds and
   stir until smooth. Alternatively, put in
   a heatproof bowl over a pan of hot
   (not boiling) water, stirring vigorously
   to break up lumps. Once smooth,
   remove from the heat.
2. Using an electric mixer, whip the
   cream until soft peaks form. Pour in
   half of the custard and fold into the
   whipped cream. Repeat with the other
   half. Once the marmalade has cooled
   to room temperature, fold in until well
   incorporated.
3. If using to fill ice cream sandwiches,
   you can spread onto the cookies
   before freezing. Otherwise spoon into
   an airtight plastic container, allowing at
   least 1cm (½in) of empty space at the
   top of the container as the mixture
   will expand as it freezes. Allow to
   freeze for at least 1 hour.

REFRESHING TREATS

At Buttercup Cake Shop, we've found a number of good uses for our ice cream beyond sandwiches. Sometimes our customers want to quench their thirst while enjoying a more filling treat. For these occasions we recommend a cupshake – your favourite cupcake blended up with vanilla ice cream and milk into a really thick milkshake. Or when you want lighter refreshment, a Cola Float usually fits the bill. And for those who want their cake and ice cream enjoyed with a spoon, we offer a Cupcake Sundae. In this section you'll find recommendations for how to get the best results for each of these treats.

COOKIES 'N' CREAM CUPSHAKE

Whoever first put together vanilla ice cream and Oreo® cookies was a genius! We think we've gone one step better at Buttercup by combining vanilla ice cream with our cookies 'n' cream cupcake, and now this is our top-selling cupshake flavour. If you are short on time, you can skip making the buttercream, and simply add two Oreo cookies and 2 tablespoons of whipped cream with the other ingredients straight into the blender.

Makes 1 large cupshake

5g (1 tsp) butter, softened
2 tbsp icing sugar
2 tbsp whipped cream
2 Oreo® cookies, crushed
2 large scoops of softened Vanilla Ice Cream (see p. 112 or premium store-bought)
1 Chocolate Cupcake (see p. 109 or store-bought)
150ml (½ cup) full-fat or semi-skimmed cold milk, plus 2 tbsp if required

1. In a small bowl using a mini whisk, mix the softened butter and icing sugar until smooth. Fold in the whipped cream and crushed cookies then set aside.
2. Ensure the ice cream is taken out of the freezer far enough in advance to soften it to scooping texture. Add two large, rounded scoops of ice cream to a blender. The scoopfuls should be well packed without pockets of air or you will end up with a cupshake that is too liquid.
3. Cut the cupcake into quarters, remove from the paper case and add to the blender. Use a large spoon to push down the cake as much as possible. This step is necessary to ensure the cake grinds up rather than remaining in chunks. Pour the cold milk over the cupcake. Add the buttercream mixture.
4. Place the top securely on the blender and turn on to low speed for 20 seconds. Switch to high speed until a normal milkshake consistency is achieved. Turn off the blender and use a spoon to check any chunks of cake at the bottom have broken up.
5. If you find the milkshake is too thick to mix properly, you can add up to 2 tablespoons more of cold milk. Do not add more than this as it will be too liquid. Pour into a serving cup, leaving 3mm (⅛in) empty at the top. Serve immediately with a thick straw and long spoon. (The mixture will be too thick to enjoy through a thin straw!)

CHOCOLATE CUPSHAKE

When you're peckish but also wanting refreshment, this cupshake will fit the bill. A combination of milkshake and cupcake, the blend is truly decadent! At Buttercup our cupcakes are always thickly iced with chocolate buttercream. For a simpler treat, you can use an un-iced cupcake. Avoid sugarpaste, though, as it doesn't blend well.

Makes 1 large cupshake

2 large scoops of softened Vanilla Ice Cream (see p. 112 or premium store-bought)
1 Chocolate Cupcake (see p. 109 or store-bought)
150ml (½ cup) full-fat or semi-skimmed cold milk, plus 2 tbsp if required

1. Ensure the ice cream is taken out of the freezer far enough in advance to soften it to scooping texture. Add two large, rounded scoops of ice cream to a blender. The scoopfuls should be well packed without pockets of air or you will end up with a cupshake that is too liquid.
2. Take your chosen cupcake. Remove any sugarpaste or non-edible decoration. Cut it into quarters, remove from the paper case and add to the blender. With a large spoon, push down the cake as much as possible. This step is necessary to ensure the cake grinds up rather than remaining in chunks. Pour the cold milk over the cupcake.
3. Place the top securely on the blender and turn on to low speed for 20 seconds. Switch to high speed until a normal milkshake consistency is achieved. Turn off the blender and use a spoon to check any chunks of cake at the bottom have broken up.
4. If you find that the milkshake is too thick to mix properly, you can add up to 2 tablespoons more of cold milk. Do not add more than this or it will be too liquid.
5. Pour into a serving cup, leaving 3mm (⅛ in) empty at the top. Serve immediately with a thick straw and a long spoon. (The mixture will be too thick to enjoy through a thin straw!)

CUPCAKE SUNDAE

This treat will take you back to childhood birthday parties, as it combines the favourites of cake and ice cream ... plus the added indulgence of an easy home-made chocolate sauce!

Makes 1 sundae

60g (¼ cup) plain (semi-sweet) chocolate chips
40ml (2 tbsp + 2 tsp) whipping cream
1 Chocolate Cupcake (see p. 109 or store-bought)
2 large scoops of softened Vanilla Ice Cream (see p. 112 or premium store-bought)
1 tbsp chocolate sprinkles and/or flakes (optional)

1. To prepare the chocolate sauce, combine the chocolate chips and cream in a very small microwave-proof bowl, and microwave on high power for 10–20 seconds or until the cream is hot and the chocolate starts to melt. Stir until the chocolate is completely melted and the mixture is thick and smooth. If necessary, return to the microwave for another 10 seconds or until melted. Stir well until no lumps remain. Alternatively, you can put in a small heatproof bowl over a pan of hot (not boiling) water and stir constantly until completely melted.
2. Set the mixture aside and allow to thicken slightly. (If it becomes too stiff to serve, you can re-heat for a couple of seconds in the microwave or over the pan of hot water.) Remove the paper wrapper from the cupcake and put upright in a sundae glass or small serving bowl.
3. Take a piping bag with a toothed icing nozzle, and fold over the top of the bag around your cupped hand. Fill with two scoops of semi-soft ice cream. Working quickly, push the ice cream down towards the nozzle, working any air bubbles to the top.
4. Gently squeeze the ice cream around the edge of the cupcake, starting from the outside and working your way in a spiral towards the centre. The ice cream should completely cover the cupcake. End with a flourish in the centre as you pull away the piping nozzle.
5. With a spoon, drizzle the chocolate sauce over the ice cream. Add sprinkles or flakes if desired and serve immediately with a sturdy spoon.

COLA FLOAT

On the one hand it seems a bit silly, really, to include a 'recipe' for a cola float especially as it's only got two ingredients. But the younger generation in particular isn't very familiar with them, so at the shops we get asked about them a lot. A treat that was especially popular in the American malt shops in the 1950s, our cola floats have proven to be very popular today with all ages. We prefer regular cola; however, diet cola can be substituted and still makes a delicious treat!

Makes 1 large cola float

1 large scoop + 1 tbsp Vanilla Ice Cream (see p. 112 or premium store-bought)
330ml (1½ cups) cola, very cold

1. Place the scoop of ice cream in a tall glass, then add the separate tablespoonful. The tablespoonful will float separately to the top when served, so that you can enjoy the wonderful combination of creamy ice cream and effervescent coke right from the first mouthful!
2. Tip the glass by 45 degrees, then very very slowly pour in the cola, aiming to hit just below the rim so as to control the amount of foam. The key to success is in slow and careful pouring, so take your time.
3. When the foam reaches the top of the glass, pause if necessary before topping up with cola. You should be able to get all or most of it into one large glass. Serve with either a straw-spoon or a separate tall straw and long spoon.

   TIP: Other people swear by the method of adding the cola to the glass first then the ice cream. I call this method the 'cannon bomb', and it can lead to uncontrolled foaming and over-flowing. So while definitely quicker, adopt it at your own risk!

INDEX

aloha sandwiches 16–17
amaretto biscuits 99
  elderflower amarettos 36–7
apple cookies, grated 91
  apple pie à la mode 32

banana
  banoffee sandwiches 27
  bread 106–7
  bread sandwiches 27, 39
  monkey sandwiches 20
  split sandwiches 39
Beverly Hills cookies 98
  Beverly Hills darlings 18–19
bounty bites 22–3
brownies see butterscotch brownies,
  chewy chocolate brownies
butterscotch brownies 84
  butterscotchies 21
butterscotch sauce 12

caramel snickerdoodle-doo 12–13
celebration cake sandwiches 75
chewy chocolate brownies 82–3
chocolate
  banana split sandwiches 39
  Beverly Hills cookies 18–19, 98
  candy crush 57
  chewy brownie sandwiches 14–15, 20,
    24–5, 50, 52–3, 58–9, 62–3, 76–7
  chewy brownies 82–3
  chip cookies, all-American 88
  chip cookies, all-American, sandwiches
    16–17, 72–3
  chip stars 72–3
  cookies 'n' cream cupshake 118–19

cupcake sundae 121
cupcakes 109, 118–21
cupshake 120
hazelnut sandwiches 24–5
ice cream 112
ice cream sandwiches 16–17, 22–5,
  52–3, 56, 76–7
marshmallow brownies 50
meringues 86
tin roof cookies 56, 100–1
see also mocha...; white chocolate chip
  cookies
coconut macaroons 96–7
  bounty bites 22–3
cola float 122–3
cookies 'n' cream cupshake 118–19
cupcakes, chocolate 109, 118–21
cupshakes
  chocolate 120
  cookies 'n' cream 118–19

elderflower amarettos 36–7
equipment 9

fig (pig), fresh, sandwiches 34–5
flocked trees 68–9
fruitcake cookies 102–3
  fruitcake delights 74

ginger cookies, soft 92
  ginger lemon gems 28–9
graveyard coffins 76–7

hazelnut chocolate sandwiches 24–5

ingredients 9

lemon ice cream 115
  lemon creams 38

ginger lemon gems 28–9

macaroons, coconut 22–3, 96–7
madeleines
  marmalade 44–5
  zesty 105
marmalade
  bear sandwiches 58–9
  ice cream 115
  ice cream sandwiches 44–5, 58–9, 74
  madeleines 44–5
marshmallow
  banana split sandwiches 39
  chocolate brownies 50
  s'more sandwiches 52–3
mascarpone ice cream 114
  mascarpone pumpkin sandwiches 46–7
  merry drums 64–5
melon sorbet butterflies 42–3
meringues
  chocolate 86
  rose 40–1
  vanilla 86–7
merry drums 64–5
mint chip valentines 62–3
mocha
  cookies 26, 104
  ice cream 114
  ice cream sandwiches 16–17, 26
  loaf 108
  loaf sandwiches 75
  mocha morsels 26
monkey sandwiches 20

oatmeal cookies, soft 89
  sandwiches using 38, 57

peaches 'n' cream 33

peanut(s)
  monkey sandwiches 20
  peanut butter bites 56
  peanut butter dream 14–15
  tin roof cookies 56, 100–1
pumpkin spice cookies 94–5
  pumpkin mascarpone sandwiches 46–7

rose meringues 40–1

s'more sandwiches 52–3
snickerdoodle cookies 85
  caramel snickerdoodle-doo 12–13
sorbet, melon, butterflies 42–3

teddies, white chocolate chip 51
tin roof cookies 100–1
  peanut butter bites 56

vanilla
  ice cream 112
  ice cream cola float 122–3
  ice cream cupcake sundae 121
  ice cream cupshakes 118–20
  ice cream sandwiches 12–13, 18–21, 27,
    32, 57
  meringue sandwiches 40–1
  meringue 86–7
  rolled cookie sandwiches 33–5, 42–3,
    64–5, 68–9
  rolled cookies 80–1

white chocolate chip cookies 93
  white chocolate chip teddies 51

zesty madeleines 105

ACKNOWLEDGEMENTS

Kate Shaw, my agent, who lends focus
and leads me patiently and thoughtfully
through unknown territory. Sydney Francis
of Haldane Mason for bringing the pieces
together at an early stage and allowing the
project to blossom. To Imogen Fortes and
Roxanne Benson-Mackey at Ebury Press
who had the vision to take on the project
and who made sure it saw the light of
day. A huge 'thank you' to the rest of the
brilliant publishing team at Ebury who lent
their expertise and support.

Ione Walder, our project editor, and
Friederike Huber, our designer, who have
a wonderful 'eye' for ensuring everyone's
work is put in the best light.

William Reavell, our talented
photographer; Denise Smart our food
stylist (whose sandwiches are always
even); Jessica Georgiades, our prop stylist;
and Lucy Harrison in Production.

My husband, Chuck, and daughters
Audrey and Amelia, who willingly tested
and provided lots of encouragement.

A big 'thank you' to my circle of
friends, family and Buttercup Cake Shop
colleagues (past and present) who share a
passion for delicious and indulgent treats.

A special thanks to my sisters and good
friends, who over the years have shared
their enthusiasm, tips and recipes for
lovely home-baked cookies, cakes, and
other wonders.

Donna Egan founded the Buttercup Cake Shop, London's first cupcakery, in 2006. Its original location in London's Kensington was soon joined by two outlets: in Westfield London and Kent, making Buttercup the first London cupcake-seller to infiltrate the heart of England, residence to many avid home bakers. In 2011, Buttercup opened its fourth outlet on the site of the UK 2012 Olympics in the new Westfield Stratford City – the largest shopping centre in Europe. Buttercup has been recognised across the press by titles including *Time Out, Metro, Daily Mail, Financial Times,* Condé Nast's *Brides,* and *British Baker,* as well as being featured on Rachel Allen's TV show, *Bake.*

Buttercup began selling ice cream sandwiches and cupshakes in Spring 2011.

They proved instantly popular to customers of all ages and became the impetus for writing this book.

Donna combines a corporate background in consumer marketing with her role as a 'mum who bakes'. Originally from California, she has lived in London for 12 years, as well as previously having lived and worked in Mexico and France. Today she lives in South London with her husband and two daughters, aged 14 and 9, who also love to bake.